· · · A · · ·
GLASGOW
KEEK SHOW

GLIMPSES OF CITY LIFE

*

FRANK WORSDALL

RICHARD DREW PUBLISHING

FIRST PUBLISHED 1981
© FRANK WORSDALL 1981

PUBLISHED BY
RICHARD DREW PUBLISHING LIMITED
20 PARK CIRCUS GLASGOW G3 6BE
SCOTLAND

ISBN 0 904002 87 X

SET IN GOUDY OLD STYLE
BY HM REPROS, GLASGOW.
PRINTED AND BOUND BY
WILLIAM COLLINS SONS & CO, LTD
GLASGOW

For MOLLIE
George Gordon's great grand-daughter,
who enjoys these glimpses of the past.

ACKNOWLEDGMENTS

As always I am greatly indebted to Mr. Fisher and
the staff of the Glasgow Room of the Mitchell Library,
for their unfailing helpfulness,
and also permission to copy many of the illustrations.
I should also like to thank Ian Gallacher,
Moira Murray, and Brian Rogers
for their willing help
in the collection and copying of material.
Finally, I should like to thank John S. Burns, the publishers,
for permission to quote from my old headmaster's classic book
The Irish in Scotland.

CONTENTS

INTRODUCTION

The mention of history, with its memories of elusive dates and youthful boredom, is enough to strike terror into the bravest heart. Of course that was world history — concerned with the antics of far-off monarchs with their endless plotting and senseless battles. Naturally, it was enough to put anybody off the subject for the rest of their lives.

Now local history (hardly touched on at school) is a very different matter. It is concerned with our own ancestors, their day-to-day lives, their pleasures and sorrows, and the district in which they worked and died. Most important of all, local history is something one can get physically involved with. There are countless ways in which one can make an individual contribution, find out things which have never been noticed before, and generate a personal satisfaction which reading other people's interpretations of things can never do.

This book is an attempt to introduce the reader to two important sources of local history — contemporary accounts of events, and the recollections of the elderly. The result, the author hopes, is a lighthearted and entertaining collection of peeps or keeks at Glasgow's past, which nevertheless give an accurate account of certain aspects of life in the city during the three centuries from 1600 to 1900.

"History is merely gossip," says one of Oscar Wilde's supercilious characters. That is far too sweeping a statement to be entirely true, but, like all generalisations there is a grain of truth in it. History, after all, is about people and their attitude to their fellows and to the world around them. This book tries to illuminate these subjects. The sources are all readily available. The extracts from the Burgh records, the newspapers, journals, and books of reminiscences, can easily be consulted.

It is hoped that readers will be encouraged to look again at the subject of history, and see whether perhaps they have undervalued it as a source of pleasure as well as a serious study. The author would be very happy if it also encouraged some of our youngsters to take a greater interest in the great and fascinating city in which they live.

ANIMALS

Animal welfare, so much a feature of life today, played no part in seventeenth-century affairs. The burghers of that time had what we would consider a callous disregard for their animals' wellbeing. On the other hand one can understand the dread which drove them to pass harsh bye-laws against wandering cats and dogs, at a time when fires and epidemics were the two greatest hazards of city life. In the following century fear of rabies was added to their worries, and equally drastic measures had to be taken to prevent the spread of that disease. The eighteenth-century Glaswegian was insatiably curious and found it difficult to resist the spectacles mounted by an almost continuous procession of showmen. These shows consisted largely of *educated* animals and monsters both apparently being of absorbing interest to city dwellers but scantily provided with public amusements. Some of the exhibits were very dubious, as Senex, a more gentle and humane observer than most, records, but at least the animals seem to have given value for money. One has to disregard, of course, the whole question of the desirability of making animals perform childish tricks completely foreign to their nature simply to amuse a few unintelligent humans. Most of the other extracts are self-explanatory, although the number of assorted animals found wandering about on the city streets in the nineteenth century seems rather odd. Perhaps the large number of taverns had something to do with it!

------------------ * ------------------

MAD DOGS

The Magistrates of this Place having been inform'd that several Butchers Dogs have been lately bit by a Mad Dog, have published a proclamation discharging the Inhabitants from allowing their Dogs to appear in the Streets for the Space of 6 Weeks, unless they are muzl'd, under penalty of having them kill'd.

GLASGOW JOURNAL *10 August 1741.*

CANINE MADNESS

THE LORD PROVOST and MAGISTRATES of GLASGOW having received certain information, that a Woman and several Dogs in this city have lately been bitten by a MAD DOG, do hereby strictly prohibit and discharge all persons from letting their Dogs go loose in the city, and enjoin and require them to keep up and confine their Dogs for the space of six weeks from this date, under the penalty of FIVE SHILLINGS sterling for each offence to be paid to the informer. And in case any Dog be found going loose in the city from and after Wednesday the fourth of February next, the Town Officers are hereby requested, and all Others are authorised to kill such Dogs, and a reward of One Shilling sterling for each Dog so killed will be paid by William Watson, keeper of the Town Clerks' Chamber.

Council Chamber, 30th Jan. 1795.

GLASGOW COURIER *31 January 1795.*

————————— * —————————

BEWARE OF READING BOOKS

On Tuesday last, as an old Man was lying in the Green reading a Book, he was attack'd by the Town Bull, who tore two of his Ribs from the Back Bone, and broke his Back Bone. His Life is dispair'd of.

GLASGOW JOURNAL *21 June 1742.*

————————— * —————————

ANIMAL SHOWS

The first show that I attended took place more than eighty years ago, and was that of a white polar bear (*Ursus maritimus*). It was stationed alongside of a large tin trough or tank, filled with water, in which it had the liberty of taking a bath. It was a very fine specimen of the species, being upwards of 12 feet in length, with hair long, soft, and white. It had more of a placid than of a ferocious look, but appeared extremely uneasy at being confined, and seemed to feel that it was quite out of its natural element, which it showed by occasionally roaring dolefully, as if in distress. In order to silence it, the keeper used to dash a pailful of water in its face, which it took very kindly, and so eased its clamouring. It was not shut up in a cage, but only confined to the floor by an iron chain, which was of a length sufficient to enable it to climb into the water trough or tank at its pleasure.

GLASGOW PAST AND PRESENT *vol. III page 317.*

TO THE LOVERS OF
REAL CURIOSITIES

This is to acquaint the Nobility, Gentry, and others, that the Brother of the famous Mr. ZUCKER, a high German (who has gained such universal applause), is just come to town, and will perform at James Buchanan's, at the White Hart in the Gallowgate on Friday the 6th instant, and continue to do so every day. The door to be opened at eleven forenoon, and begin exactly half-an-hour after, and ends at one; and in the evening at half-an-hour after six, and ends at eight . . . He has brought with him the most amazing learned little Horse from Courland, whose wonderful knowledge is not to be paralleled by any animal in this kingdom, or perhaps in the whole world. As a specimen of his abilities, we shall mention the following particulars, viz. — He makes a polite and curious compliment to the Company; tells the value of anything which is shown to him; he plays at cards, and finds the place where the card is hid; shows by a watch the hour of the day, and understands arithmetic; he distinguishes Ladies from Gentlemen; he understands the Almanack, and demonstrates the day of the month; he plays at Dice, and is always sure to win; he drinks the Company's health like a human Person; his Master borrows a piece of Money of one of the Company, and throws it on the floor; the Horse takes it up and returns it to the Person that lent it; when he is told that he is to leave the empire or go to the Grand Turk he shams lame and walks about the Room as a cripple; but when he is told he shall be excused, he immediately recovers, makes his compliments on his knees, and thanks the Company. . . .

GLASGOW JOURNAL *5 January 1764.*

AN EDUCATED PIG

GLASGOW MERCURY, 9th May 1787. — Among the infinite number of curiosities hitherto offered to the inspection and attention of the public, there are none which lay so great a claim to our attention and approbation as the wonderful and astonishing performances of the "learned pig" now exhibiting in Mr. Frazer's Dancing Hall, McNair's Land, King Street, from eleven o'clock forenoon, to three in the afternoon, and from five to nine at night, where it may be seen this and every day in the ensuing week, at the expiration of which the proprietor is under engagement to set off for Edinburgh.

This most singular phenomenon is one of the many surprising instances of the ingenuity of Mr. Nicholson — a man who is possessed of an exclusive and peculiar power over the most irrational part of animated nature. Many of the first personages in the three kingdoms have been witnesses to his persevering temper and patience in the tuition of beasts, birds, etc., in a degree that has seldom fallen to the lot of human infirmity. To evince this, we need only mention his having in his lifetime taught a turtle to fetch and carry articles at his pleasure; his overcoming the timidity of a hare by making her beat a drum; his perfecting six turkey-cocks in a regular country dance; his completing a small bird in the performance of many surprising feats; his having taught three cats to strike several tunes on the dulcimer with their paws, and to imitate the Italian manner of singing; but above all, his conquering the natural obstinacy and stupidity of a pig, by teaching him to unite the letters of any person's name, to tell the number of persons present in the room and the hour and minute by any watch, &c.&c. This singular creature may justly be deemed the greatest curiosity in the kingdom, and the proprietor makes no doubt but he will give that satisfaction, and receive that approbation, from the ladies and gentlemen of this city &c.&c., which he has done in London and Edinburgh. Admittance, 6d each.

I paid my sixpence and witnessed the above-mentioned performances, which I must confess were truly very extraordinary, more especially knowing how obstinate and intractable an animal a pig is. . . .

Mons. Buffon has stated that the hog is the most impure and filthy of all animals, and is naturally stupid, inactive, and drowsy; that all its habits are gross; all its appetites nauseous; all its sensations confined to a furious lust and a brutal gluttony. It devours indiscriminately everything that comes in its way — even its own progeny, the moment after their birth. Who could fondle with pleasure such an animal, however learned?

GLASGOW PAST AND PRESENT *vol. III page 328.*

———————— * ————————

THE SAD END OF A PERFORMING FLEA

The next show that I shall take notice of was certainly a very curious one; and I believe that nothing of the kind has ever since been exhibited in Europe. We have had many shows of learned horses, learned dogs, and even learned pigs; but who nowadays, ever saw a learned flea? The very idea of the thing appears ludicrous. Nevertheless, such was the novel spectacle exhibited to our wondering citizens of olden time, as the following advertisement fully explains:—

GLASGOW JOURNAL *4th August 1763.*

THIS IS TO ACQUAINT THE CURIOUS

That there is to be exhibited by the inventor and maker, S. Boverick, from nine in the morning till eight in the evening, at the sign of the Mason's Arms, opposite the Main Guard, Trongate, at one shilling each person, the so much admired collection of Miniature Curiosities, consisting of the following pieces:—

1. An ivory chaise with four wheels, and all the proper apparatus belonging to them, turning readily on their axis together, with a man sitting on the chaise, all drawn by a flea, without any seeming difficulty, the chaisemen and flea being barely equal to a single grain.

2. A flea chained to a chain of 200 links, with a padlock and key — all weighing less than one-third of a grain. The padlock locks and unlocks. . . .

3. A landau, which opens and shuts by springs, hanging on braces, with four persons therein, two footmen behind, a coachman on the box with a dog between his legs, six horses and a postilion, all drawn by a single flea! . . .

. . . the death of this poor flea was truly comical. It took place thus, as reported to me:— A country wife, from Pollokshaws, having come to Glasgow on a market day to sell her fowls and eggs, happened to see people going into the above-mentioned show in Buchanan's Land, and, as she had made very favourable sales that day of her stock, she resolved to see the said show; accordingly, without knowing exactly what she was about to see, she paid her admission money, and directly thereafter marched up to the table on which the flea was performing its task of drawing the ivory coach and coachman. The poor woman looked only to the flea, and instantly turning down her thumb nail upon it, cracked it in a moment, exclaiming — "Filthy beast, wha could hae brought you here?" The showman, in a violent rage, seized the woman by the throat, and demanded how she dared to kill the flea. On the other hand, the astonished woman, not knowing that she had done anything wrong, exclaimed — "Losh me, man, makin' sic a wark about a flea; gif you come wi' me to the Shaws, we'll gi'e ye a peck o' them, and be muckle obliged to you for takin' them." As the woman was a widow, and possessed little or no property, Mr. Boverick thought it most prudent to put up with his loss, in place of going into a court of law for damages. In the present times, the value of a flea would be a curious question at a jury trial. The flea (*Pulex*) has six legs; nevertheless it seldom walks, but is remarkable for its agility in leaping to a height equal to 200 times that of its own body. This bloodthirsty insect, which fattens at the expense of the human species, is said to prefer the more delicate skin of young ladies, in which, with its piercer or sucker, it first makes an entrance, and then thrusts it farther into the flesh, so as to make the blood flow from the adjacent parts, and thus occasions that round red spot, with a hole in the centre, called a "flea bite". The learned flea in question, however, was not favoured with such a delicate morsel as a mouthful from the limb of a young lady, but took its meals from the plump and juicy arms of Mr. Boverick himself, who fed it carefully with his own blood, and at night kept it snugly domiciled in a little box lined with soft velvet and select silken caddis, by which attentions it came to be on friendly and intimate terms with its master.

GLASGOW PAST AND PRESENT *vol. III page 324.*

------------------------------ * ------------------------------

A COW WITH TWO HEADS

GLASGOW MERCURY *3d November 1785* . . .
Just arrived, and to be seen alive, in a commodious room near the Spoutmouth, Gallowgate, the surprising Worcestershire HEIFER, six years old, being the most curious production of nature ever exhibited in this kingdom. This very surprising creature has two heads, four horns, four eyes, four ears, four nostrils, through each of which it breathes, &c., and what is

more surprising, it takes its sustenance with both mouths at the same time. One of the heads, together with the horns, represents that of a bull, and the other that of a cow. ... The above curiosity, with several other curious beasts, alive, may be seen by any number of persons, from ten in the morning, till eight at night. Ladies or gentlemen, 1s; tradesmen, 6d; servants, 3d.

---------------- * ----------------

I paid a visit to this wonderful heifer, and certainly thought the show well worthy of the attention of *virtuosi*. One of the heads of this animal appeared to me to be perfect, and as vital as that of a healthy cow; but the other head was dull and sluggish, and hung down from the neck like an excrescence; the eyes in it were glazed and inanimated, and the expression of its countenance was that of imbecility. The animal itself, however, was pleasing to look at, and appeared very mild and gentle in its nature. I patted its perfect head, which it took very kindly, and seemed pleased with my attentions.

GLASGOW PAST AND PRESENT *vol. III page 359.*

HORSES

WANTED, at GOVAN COALERY, within one mile of Glasgow, a PERSON who will contract to keep ten gin, and six waggon horses, the horses to be delivered over to the contractor, at the beginning of his contract, and taken back at the end of it, at a valuation to be fixed by men mutually chosen, the difference being paid or received. A dwelling house, stables for twenty horses, and hayloft, all in good repair, will be found to the contractor free of rent, and, in case he chuse it, from forty to fifty acres of good land, in excellent condition, upon moderate terms. The entry to commence at Martinmas next.

Any person whom this may suit will apply to James Dunlop of Carmyle, at Glasgow, or Robert Edmiston, manager of the Coalery at Govan, when he will be informed of the terms, which are such as will make it an object to an industrious man.

GLASGOW MERCURY 6 *August 1778.*

---------------- * ----------------

NEW YEAR'S DAY IN GOVAN

Amongst the amusements of the lower classes in Glasgow in those days, perhaps the most reprehensible was the practice of shooting cocks at Govan on New-Year's Day. On the morning of that day the road to this village might have been seen crowded with idle boys and half-tipsy operatives hurrying along, armed with fowling-pieces and guns of various forms and calibres, in expectation of being able to bring home a cock to their dinner. The poor cock was tied to a stake, and had no chance of escape. The price of a shot was one penny; and whoever killed this noble bird received its carcass as the reward of his dexterity. It was curious to observe the sagacity of these birds in such trying circumstances; for, after receiving the first or second shot, they generally endeavoured to protect their heads by exposing their sides, thereby receiving the subsequent shots upon their wings. On every New-Year's Day Govan was the resort of a blackguard half-drunken mob, who, in addition to cock-shooting, passed the day at throwing the cudgel for gingerbread cakes, and the like sports, while there was free scope for all manner of thimble-rigging. It appears singular to us now how the sheriff or justices of the peace should have permitted such disgraceful scenes to be acted in our neighbourhood; but the practice of cock-shooting at Govan on New-Year's Day was an amusement of long standing, and, like other ancient bad practices, use and wont formed its apology.

GLASGOW PAST AND PRESENT *vol. II page 97.*

———————— * ————————

CAUTION

A mischievous Cow is now pasturing on the banks of the Clyde, nearly opposite to the Anderston Brewery. On Sunday evening, it attacked and had nearly gored a Lady who was walking down the riverside; and a servant maid, with a child in her arms, has been since also very much hurt.

GLASGOW COURIER 8 *October 1795.*

———————— * ————————

VISITORS IN THE RIVER

Monday last, three porpoises were caught in the Clyde at the Broomielaw; two of them were about twelve feet long, and nearly eight feet in circumference at the shoulder. It is supposed they had come this far up the river in pursuit of Salmon, which appear to be very plentiful in the river at present, as, next morning, a Govan fishing boat caught eighteen at one draught and thirteen at another.

GLASGOW COURIER 19 *June 1800.*

BEES

Just arrived in this City, the well-known JAMES BONNER, Bee Master, who was honoured with a Premium of Ten Guineas from the Highland Society of Scotland, for his skill and industry in the management of Bees. He will exhibit, for a few days only, in a commodious Room opposite the Tontine, A SWARM OF BEES, rendered tractable and easily managed; and which he will make to march along the table to the astonishment of the beholders — Will shew the Queen Bee, Bee Eggs, a Swarm of Bees in a Glass Hive, with many other Curiosities relative to these wonderful and industrious insects.

Instructions will also be given to Bee Masters, how easily the Honey may be taken from a Hive of Bees, without any recourse to the old barbarous method of destroying them, in order to obtain the Honey. A variety of new and useful Directions will likewise be given how to manage them during the different seasons of the year.

Attendance from 10 in the morning till 8 in the evening. Admittance — Ladies and Gentlemen 1s 6d — Tradesmen 6d. At same place, Orders will be taken for Living Bees, the finest Virgin Honey, Honey Comb, Bees Wax, and everything relative to the Bee Husbandry.

Where also may be had his Treatise entitled, A New Plan for speedily increasing the number of Bee Hives in Scotland, etc. J. B. returns his most grateful thanks to the Ladies, Gentlemen and others of this city and neighbourhood for the very extensive countenance he has received in his profession as a Bee-Master, a Dealer in Honey and Bee-Hives, in the sale of his Treatise on the Management of Bees, and by calling at his Room for instruction in his line; and hopes, by his small though well-meant exertions, to be instrumental in increasing the number of Bee-hives in this country, an object so much desired by persons of every description.

J. B. begs farther to state, that though he has been numerously attended for the last seven days, yet not a single individual has received a sting.

GLASGOW COURIER 29 May 1800.

[21]

A KICK IN THE TAIL

A band of desperate characters, male and female, were charged with rioting and fighting in houses of bad fame in Prince's Street. One of the females appeared with her head dreadfully cut by a blow from a bottle, inflicted by one of her profligate comrades. She was in a state of great weakness, and seemed to suffer severely from the effects of the assault. The magistrate directed her to be taken to the Royal Infirmary, and furnished her with an admission line; while he sentenced the brutal assailant to sixty days confinement in Bridewell. The rest of the party were dismissed, with the exception of the reputed landlord of one of the houses, who was detained for farther enquiry. Some merriment was excited in Court by the statement of Serjeant Sharpe, that he had found, on one occasion, in the house of this worthy, up one or two pair of stairs, among other animals, six females and a donkey, all nestling together with the utmost apparent comfort.

GLASGOW ARGUS 8 May 1834.

———————— * ————————

A LATE WINDOW SHOPPER

On Wednesday last, a watchman apprehended a cow which was straying at unseasonable hours in Sauchiehall-Street. In coming along to the office leading the beast by the string of his clappers attached to a horn, it suddenly took fright, and bolted off, carrying the rattles along with it, the noise of which so accelerated its motion that the policeman was soon distanced, and neither the cow nor the clappers have since been heard of.

GLASGOW HERALD 15 June 1835.

ARRIVAL OF THE RHINOCEROS

THE Inhabitants of Glasgow and its Vicinity are respectfully informed, that the RHINOCEROS, which cost the Proprietor of the Liverpool Zoological Gardens One Thousand Guineas, is now arrived in this City, and is exhibiting at No. 14 Virginia Street, opposite the Glasgow Union Bank, adjoining Mr. Donald's Sale Rooms.

Admittance, One Shilling.

GLASGOW HERALD 4 December 1835.

LOST AND FOUND

DOG LOST

Stolen or Strayed from Hillhead, this Morning,
A YOUNG BLACK NEWFOUNDLAND DOG with a White
Spot on the Breast. Answers to the name of "Tartar".
Any Person having found him, is requested to return him to Mr.
Campbell's Stables, 14, Main Street: or to the Police Office, where
they will receive a Reward.
If found in anyone's possession after this notice they will be
prosecuted.

Glasgow 6th Oct. 1848.

GLASGOW HERALD 9 October 1848.

———————— * ————————

CITY OF GLASGOW POLICE

FOUND, in Cambridge Street, on the 24th inst., a WHITE
HORSE, which will be Sold to defray Expenses unless claimed
within Three Days from this date.

> JOHN MACWHANNELL, Custodier.

Central Police Chambers, Glasgow.
26th July 1864.

GLASGOW HERALD 27 July 1864.

———————— * ————————

FOUND, a BLACK SHEEP, at 251, Duke Street. If not claimed in
Three Days, will be Sold to defray expenses.
Apply at Mrs. Paul's, at the above address.

GLASGOW HERALD 29 May 1865.

———————— * ————————

TERRA INCOGNITA

For myself, I make the shameful admission that until I was nearer
thirty than twenty I had never walked the few miles to Bearsden. It
is true that at the tender age of nine, accompanied by my younger
brother, I set out to accomplish the feat, both of us being inspired by
the belief that we should see the bear; but, having eaten our picnic
on a field at Kirklee, scarce a mile from home, we decided to return
thither and go another day. We did set out another day, but this
time we had not gone far when we met a man driving a pig (fancy a
pig today on Great Western Road!) who kindly accepted our
company, cut us useful wands from a convenient tree, and later put
us on a car, with pennies in our paws, so that eventually we came
home, full of pride and glory, the bear forgotten.

I REMEMBER J J Bell. 1932. *page 51.*

EDUCATION

After the reprehensibly frivolous tone of the first chapter, it is appropriate that the second should be on a wholly serious topic — and what could be more serious than education? The Scottish system of schooling from the seventeenth century until the passing of the Education Act of 1872 was pretty haphazard. Primary schools were under the jurisdiction of the Kirk Sessions, and secondary education was only available in the larger towns, where it was controlled by the Town Council. Glasgow, of course, had in addition, its University. This was dependant upon government funds and private benefactions, and it was extremely lucky to receive such a magnificent gift as the Hunter bequest to enable it to set up a first-class museum. There were private schools, of course, particularly in the 18th century, and these included such ex-curricular subjects as music, dancing, and cookery. Robert McNair's bright idea of combating juvenile delinquency (I didn't think it had been invented then!) by means of an educational workhouse, was clearly not a purely philanthropic measure and its promoter had high hopes of sizable profits. I wonder if it would work today?

Joseph Lancaster (1778-1838) was the first to introduce new methods of teaching in the city with new-fangled ideas like playgrounds, and he was greeted with enormous enthusiasm. Unfortunately this did not last very long and within a decade his much-praised schools were up for sale. Following the 1872 Act, which made primary education compulsory, Glasgow was divided among seven area Boards all of which erected new buildings. The most progressive Board was Govan which included much of the south side and also Partick and Hillhead on the north. Its schools were vastly superior with such mod-cons as swimming baths. Victorian prudery, however, could not be evaded, and the Govan Board boasted of their buildings which managed, by means of a superfluity of doors and staircases, to completely separate the boys from the girls. One wonders whether they realised that if carried to its logical conclusion, this scheme would only too effectively solve all the Board's problems!

*Class distinction in education —
the Mechanics' Institution and Andersons' University.*

A NEW GRAMMAR SCHOOL

The provest, bailleis, and counsale ordanit maister Johnne Blakburne and Thomas Pettigrew to aggre, contract with, and end with the masounes, wrychtis, sclateris, for bigging of the Grammer Schole as gud chaipe as thai can, and the provest, bailleis and counsall and thesaurer for the tyme to releve thame, and that with all diligence.

EXTRACTS FROM THE BURGH RECORDS *22 December 1600.*

TRUANCY IN THE 17th CENTURY

The provest, bailleis, and counsell, vpone complante maid be the said maister Johnne as maister of the Grammer Scole, and be the dekinis and maisteris of craftis, and certain vtheris nychtbouris of this town, vpone the grit and commoun abuse done be scolleris and printiciss towardis thame selfis and thair maisteris in haunting the yardis quhair the alie bowlis, Frenche Kylis, and glaikis ar usit, in withdrawing thameselfis fra the scole and thair maisteris seruice, to thair grit hurt and deboscherie baith of printiciss and scolleris, besyde the grit skaith and hurt done be thame to the nychtbouris yardis lyand nixt and ewest to the yardis quhair the pastymes foirsaid ar hauntit and vsit, in breking thair treis and distroying of thair herbis and seidis sawin in the saidis yardis; for remeid quhairof it is statute and ordanit that all sik personis quha hes the saidis aleis and yardis, and quhairintill the saidis pastymes ar vsit, that they nor nane of thame resaif in the saidis yardis to play at the saidis pastymes ony scoller or printeis, beger, or deboschit personis in tyme cuming, vndir payne of ten pund how oft they do in the contrar, and that they permit nane to play in the saidis yardis at nane of the saidis pastymes vpone the Sabboth day, forrow none nor eftir none, vndir the payne foirsaid; and that the maister of the Grammer Scole ordane his scollerris to prepair thair bowis for the archerie to thair pastyme.

EXTRACTS FROM THE BURGH RECORDS *14 April 1610.*

A MUSIC SCHOOL

The said day the proueist bailyeis and counsell aggreit with James Sanderis to instruct the haill bairnes within this burghe that is putt to his schole musik for ten schillingis ilk quarter to himselff and fourtie penneis to his man, and thairfoir the saidis proueist and bailyeis dischairges all vthir scholaris within this burghe to teache musik in tyme cuming during thair will allanerlie.

EXTRACTS FROM THE BURGH RECORDS *15 July 1626.*

. . . and now seing that the musik schooll is altogidder dekayit within this burgh, to the grait discredit of this citie and discontentment of sindrie honest men within the same who hes bairnes whom they wold have instructit in that art, and that Duncane Birnet, who sumtyme of befoir teatchit musik thairin, quhairupon the saidis provest, bailyeis, and counsall convenit the said James Sanderis befoir thame, and efter deliberatioun thairanent they, with consent of the said James Sanderis (in respect of the former act sett doun in his favouris,) hes grantit licence to the said Duncane Birnett to tak vp ane musik schooll within this brugh during thair will and pleasouris, he taking fra the toun barnes suche skollegis as is contenit in the act sett doun of befoir in favouris of the said James Sanderis.

EXTRACTS FROM THE BURGH RECORDS 5 *May* 1638.

STUDENT GRANTS

Ordaines Robert Alexander, thesaurer, to pay to each of the three youth students afternamed, viz., John Howison, son to umquhill John Howison, tayleor, James Cullane, son to umquhill James Cullane, maltman, and Robert Crawfurd, son to Robert Crawfurd, maltman, to each of them twelve pounds Scotts, to help them to buy books and to encourage them in their studies.

EXTRACTS FROM THE BURGH RECORDS 13 *September* 1698.

A DANCING SCHOOL

The magistrates and towne cownsell conveened, they upon a supplicatione given in be John Smith, danceing master, allowe and permitt the said John to teach danceing within this burgh, with and under the provisions and conditions underwritten, viz., that he shall behave himselfe soberly, teach at seasonable hours, keep noe balls, and that he shall so order his teaching that there shall be noe promiscuows danceing of yowng men and yowng women togither, bot that each sex shall be tawght be themselves, and that the one sex shall be dismised and be owt of his howse befor the other enter therein, and if the said John transgress in any of these appoynts the magistrates to putt him out of this burgh.

EXTRACTS FROM THE BURGH RECORDS 11 *November* 1699.

A WORKHOUSE FOR THE UNEMPLOYED

Robert McNair, merchant weaver, gave in the signed proposal following, that he having had under consideration to find out some proper method for employing idle persons and in some measure to be serviceable in providing them in work and free them from being a burden upon the place, has now come to a resolution and has determined, upon his own charge and expences, to purchase a piece of ground next adjacent to his oun lands, on the south side of the Tronegate, and for that purpose to build therupon a house with tuo storys and garretts of fifty six foot in length and sixteen foot in breadth, and when built, which he designs to begin on or before the month of March next, and against that time to be providing matterials for the building, and so soon as the building is finished to execute and employ the same as follows, vizt. :— in the garrets one hundred spinners to be imployed and put therin; in the story below men servants at different employments, such as weavers, warpers, winders, confectioners of different kinds to be employed and kept therin; and the ground story to be execute and employed as follows, vizt., a part of it vaulted and to be applyed for employing hecklers, lint buffers, clay searchers and bakers, and the remainder of the ground story to be made in separat apartments for dressing of victuals and providing the workers in their dyet. That considering there are many idle boys and girls in the city, and others who have no title to frequent the same, who committ bad practices and by their practices are corrupted in their morals, and that there are dayly complaints from time to time made by the inhabitants to the magistrats against such criminals who upon conviction are imprisoned and others sent to the correction house for their amendment, but so it is that upon their being liberate and that they have been brought up to no handycraft they return to their former practices and become nuisances and a scandal to the place, the said Robert McNair humbly proposes to the honourable magistrates to receive into his workhouse all such delinquents of boys, girls and others as they shall deliver to him, and furnish and employ them in work and train up and instruct them therein and furnish them in bed, board and cloathing, upon his oun expences, and demand no more than the benefite of their work, untill such time as they be capable and give proof of earning their oun bread and promoteing industry, and that such workers in his workhouse may be under discipline and correction in relation to their work, behaviour, carriage and morals, he proposes to provide an overseer, such a person as shall be agreeable and acceptable to the magistrats, to whom he shall be accountable for his management from time to time and be subject to their orders, and the overseer to be provided and maintained upon the said Robert McNair's charge; all which he obliges himself to fulfill and perform in every point as he has above proposed, and that at the sight and to the satisfaction of the magistrats. . . .

Which proposals being heard and considered by the magistrats and council they approve therof, and recommend to the magistrats

[28]

in giving their assistance and concurrence in delivering over to the said Robert McNair delinquents for the purpose forsaid, in so far as they are authorised by law.

EXTRACTS FROM THE BURGH RECORDS *1 September 1747.*

THE FIRST HUNTERIAN MUSEUM

We formerly noticed, that, in August, 1804, the Principal and Professors of the university of Glasgow, together with the Dean of Faculties, laid the foundation stone of the building intended for the reception of the *Hunterian Museum*. We can now mention, that an elegant building for that valuable Museum is now finished, that the greatest part of the articles belonging to it have already arrived, and that the remainder are soon expected. Such of the Students in this University as direct their attention to Medicine, cannot fail to derive much information, particularly relative to Anatomy, from the Anatomical Preparations in that Museum. Dr. Hunter, in his Introductory Lectures, which were published, has stated, that *"he had collected such an Anatomical Apparatus as was never brought together in any age or century"*. This celebrated Collection, now belonging to the University of Glasgow, no doubt must contribute greatly to promote the celebrity of Glasgow as a Medical School.

GLASGOW HERALD *11 September 1807.*

THE LANCASTRIAN SYSTEM

By the system of Joseph Lancaster, paradoxical as it may appear above one thousand children may be taught and governed by one Master only, at an expence now reduced to *five shillings per annum, each child*; and supposed still capable of further reduction. The average time for instruction, in Reading, Writing and Arithmetic, is twelve months. Among many other advantages which distinguish this system, is a new method of teaching to Read and Spell; whereby one Book worth Seven Shillings, will serve to teach Five Hundred Boys, who, in the usual method would require Five Hundred Books, worth above Twenty-five Pounds. The improvement is three times greater by the new method than the old. Any boy, who can read, can teach Arithmetic with the certainty of a mathematician, although he knows nothing about it himself.

GLASGOW HERALD *20 November 1807.*

Friday the foundation stone of the Gorbals Public School, upon an improved plan (being the first public school of the kind in Scotland) was laid by Robert Ferrie Esq., chief magistrate of Gorbals, in presence of David Niven and William Mills Esq., resident magistrates, the Rev. James McLean, the members of the Committee and a number of the other subscribers to the School, who walked in procession from the Court House in Gorbals, preceded by the band of the Argyllshire Militia. After the ceremony, Bailie Ferrie addressed the company and a numerous assemblage of spectators, in a most appropriate speech, setting forth the advantages that may be expected to arise from such an Institution, not only to the present, but to future generations. The School is situated on the west side of Portugal Street, in a free, airy situation, and is to be built to a plan both elegant and commodious.

GLASGOW HERALD 8 October 1810.

———————— * ————————

The public are hereby respectfully informed that the East Lancasterian School, for the teaching of Reading, Writing, and Arithmetic, has just been opened for the reception of pupils, by Mr. William Collins, in a Room adjoining Mr. Dunn's Cotton Mill, Tobago Street, Calton; and that the West School will be opened on Tuesday first, the 6th inst., by Mr. William Boyd (late of Greenock) in a Room connected with Mr. Houldsworth's Cotton Mill, Anderston. These places have been granted by their respective proprietors, for temporary accommodation, till the proper School Houses, which are intended each to contain 800 scholars can be built and furnished. The School House in the East is contracted for and is expected to be ready for entrance about Candlemas next. Respecting that in the West, all that can be said at present is that there will not be a day's unnecessary delay. In the meantime, the Children will be taught, as far as the nature of the accommodation will permit, on the same principles as afterwards, and every attention will be paid to their improvement: one design of beginning in this way being to prepare boys and girls, who may show superior abilities, to act as Monitors in the Schools when they come to be more extended. . . .

GLASGOW HERALD 5 November 1810.

———————— * ————————

Wednesday, a public dinner was given in the Great Room of the Black Bull Inn in this city. . . . After five months travelling in Ireland for the purpose of introducing his system into that country, Mr. Lancaster quitted it on the 1st current, returning to London through Scotland, for the sake of visiting Glasgow and Edinburgh, but, unwilling to lose a useful hour, lectured at Ayr on the 4th, and Kilmarnock on the 5th; at both towns being cordially welcomed by the Magistrates and respectable inhabitants. On the 7th he visited the Schools which bear the name of Lancasterian in Glasgow, and reported their state in a general meeting of the Directors of the Institutions here, who, highly to their honour, were convened, to meet with and show every kind attention which the friends of humanity and knowledge in this city could evince, to a benevolent stranger.

He recommended measures, calculated to gratify their warmest wishes, and those of the public, by speedily introducing the system completely into the Schools here, and he pointed out others, which, if properly executed, would have the most beneficial effect, in extending the economy and other benefits of the system into every place in the west of Scotland, where it might be required. The importance and obvious advantages of these propositions, induced the Directors of the Institution, to call a general meeting of the Society for the consideration of them. In the interim, Mr. Lancaster went to Paisley and Greenock. . . . He returned to Glasgow: and one of the Schools in this city, having formerly been far from prosperous, the system not having been properly acted upon by the teacher who had the charge of it, he held a meeting of near 1,000 persons in the Calton School Room, and delivered a lecture, calculated to give a good impression of the plan, to the parents of the children. He was as well received and as well attended to, as could be wished. . . . The instant the lecture was over, he set off, by the Mail, to Edinburgh, in order to make his arrangements in person, for a lecture there: and found a general meeting of the Committee of the Lancasterian School in that place, had appointed a public dinner at Oman's Hotel, to welcome his arrival. . . . Having completed his arrangements for Lecturing in Edinburgh, he again returned hither, to lecture in the Theatre, where he again met a cheerful auditory who gave him a most hearty welcome. The Master of the Calton School appeared on the stage with a detachment of fine little fellows, who illustrated part of the plan, by their evolutions. The lad who attended them, and gave the commands, is one of Mr. Lancaster's apprentices from London: an orphan, who has been 5 years with Mr. Lancaster; and though only 14 years of age, has organised several Schools on his system, and contributed most materially to their success — and whose services, in the Calton School, will not soon be forgotten. Robert Owen Esq., of New Lanark was in the chair. . . .

GLASGOW HERALD *20 April 1812.*

GLASGOW LANCASTERIAN
SCHOOL SOCIETY

The Barony of Gorbals Lancasterian School was opened on Monday the 22nd of February, for the admission of scholars. The Schoolroom has been completely fitted up with telegraphic signals, and all the other apparatus necessary for the full application of the Lancasterian plan of teaching. It is neat, commodious, and comfortable, in an uncommon degree, and from the experience and respectable character of the teacher, Mr. Loutit, and his thorough acquaintance with the plan to be followed, it is hoped he will meet with desired encouragement.

Hours of attendance for the day school, from 10 to 12 and from 1 to 3. Wages (for reading, writing and arithmetic) 3s a quarter, to be paid monthly in advance.

Hours for the evening school, which is intended chiefly for children and young persons who are employed through the day in cotton mills, and other public works, from 8 to half past 9. Wages 1s 6d a quarter, to be paid also monthly in advance.

GLASGOW HERALD *1 March 1813.*

———————— * ————————

TO BE SOLD LANCASTERIAN SCHOOL,
GORBALS

That large and handsome building and offices in Portugal Street of Gorbals . . . with the area of ground surrounding the same. The building was erected for a Public School, is of the best materials and workmanship, extends 100 feet along the street by 37 feet deep, and is fit for various useful purposes. . . .

GLASGOW HERALD *14 May 1821.*

———————— * ————————

GLASGOW GRAMMAR SCHOOL

THE FALSE and SLANDEROUS ACCOUNT of this Establishment which appeared in the SCOTS TIMES of Saturday last, will, in a day or two, be Disproved by Official Documents.

GLASGOW HERALD *8 October 1827.*

GLASGOW HERALD *12 July 1875.*

———————— * ————————

OPENING OF HILLHEAD PUBLIC SCHOOL

The large and handsome school which has been erected at Sardinia Terrace, Hillhead, by the Govan (Parish) School Board was opened for inspection on Saturday afternoon. A large number of the ratepayers of the district availed themselves of the opportunity of inspecting the new structure. Amongst those present during the course of the day were Mr. Alexander Stephen, Chairman, and Mr. Taylor and Mr. Crichton, members of the Govan School Board; Mr. J. N. Cuthbertson, of the Glasgow School Board; Rev. Mr. Laidlaw and Rev. Mr. Hislop.

The new school occupies a site, with buildings and playgrounds, of 3535 square yards. It has a frontage of 105 feet and a depth of 86 feet. The school-rooms are on three floors, and owing to the declivity of the street — there is a basement of 12 feet ceiling on the north side above the level of the street. This basement is occupied at the front by the dwelling-house of the janitor, behind which is a large covered playground open to the boys' playground, and through which is the access to the boys' staircase. The girls and infants enter by the upper gateway at the south side of the school. The outside passage between the girls' and infants' entrances is roofed over with iron and glass, and a covered way communicates with the outside offices. In the three floors of the building — measured at the ordinary rate of 8 square feet for infants and 10 square feet for each of the others — there is accommodation for 1429 scholars; but as the upper floor is intended for auxiliary purposes, such as sewing, drawing, also science lecture-room and laboratory, the measurement of the upper floor has only been taken as 20 square feet each, thus reducing the maximum number of scholars proposed to be accommodated to 1180. The total cost of the building will be about £11,000. The ground floor is chiefly occupied by the infant and initiatory departments, occupying five rooms. On this floor are a large cloak-room, and luncheon-room for girls, and a separate cloak-room for infants, as also private room for head mistress and room adjoining front entrance for head master, who can from his room communicate by speaking tubes with each of his assistant masters. Cloak-room for boys and rooms for assistant teachers are placed on an entresol floor.

On the first floor are the junior and senior departments, each of three large rooms, two of which in each department are divided by movable partitions. The senior rooms are furnished with Bennet's dual desks. A large lecture-room, with gallery and apparatus-rooms for science classes, is provided on the upper floor, also a working laboratory for 20 students. These are fitted up in accordance with the requirements of the Science and Art Department of South Kensington. A notable feature in the school is that there are separate doors for boys and girls to separate stairs from each room on all the floors. This has been only partly accomplished in other schools. The large, well-lighted double staircase, is indeed, the feature of the school. It is handsomely decorated with full-size plaster copies, 40 feet by 3 feet, of the frieze of the Parthenon of Athens, commonly termed the Elgin Marbles, which are of a highly educative value. On the upper landings in the staircases are placed glass cases for natural history specimens. The heating and ventilation will be unusually efficient, mechanical power being applied for the first time in the district to ventilation purposes — a 48 in. fan, "Aland's" patent, is driven by a 2 h.p. "Otto" gas engine, placed in a chamber on upper floor, to which ducts are led from all the rooms, and the vitiated air extracted. Corresponding ducts introduce fresh air from a chamber in the basement, while the air can be warmed by hot-water pipes in cold weather. Hot-water pipes on the low-pressure principle are carried through all the rooms. The building has been erected from the designs of Messrs. H and D Barclay, architects; Mr. Samuel Preston, from the Board Office, being Clerk of Works. . . .

The school is to be under the charge of Mr. Edward E. Macdonald, who so successfully conducted the Albert Road School under the Govan Board.

GLASGOW HERALD 13 April 1885.

NEW BOARD SCHOOL FOR GOVAN

This evening Mr. John Wilson, M.P., will open Lorne Street Public School, which has been erected by Govan Parish School Board. The new school is admirably situated, fronting a large open public space at the east end of the new Govan Road, on the south of the Cessnock Docks. The site was acquired from the Clyde Trustees and consists of 4245 square yards, of which 3102 yards are building ground. The price was £2 per square yard for the net building ground, or at the rate of 29s for the whole. The building is three storeys in height, and has the infant department on the ground floor, and the classrooms for the standards upon the first and second floors, the total accommodation being 1414 scholars. The infant department has a very large central hall, paved with noiseless wood block flooring. The hall is intended for musical drill, the infant school-rooms opening upon it with sliding partitions. All the classrooms are fitted up with the most recent improvements and appliances. The features of this school are, however, the complete system of heating and mechanical ventilation, the possession of a first-class swimming pond and gymnasium, a technical workshop, a cookery school, and a complete laundry. In the completeness of these departments this school building is understood to be in advance of anything hitherto done. The swimming pond is 50 feet long by 27 feet broad, with necessary washing-room and dressing boxes. To heat the bath a steam boiler is used, and the heating has been so satisfactorily accomplished that not the slightest vibration is felt in the process. The steam is also used for the heating of the classrooms, the whole of the pipes, however, being in the underground passages. A 72 inch fan, driven by a steam engine, forces the tempered air into all rooms in such volume as can change the air every ten minutes without perceptible draught. The boys' workshop has 30 working benches, and a corresponding number of drawing-desks to carry out the practical and theoretical lessons together. A laundry is being built above the girls' play-shed. It will be provided with tubs for 16 pupils, also steam drying closets and ironing tables.

The school is built of Locharbriggs red stone in the Italian style of architecture, of bold and simple design, from plans by Messrs H. & D. Barclay, architects, Glasgow, and under their superintendence, and that of the Board's Master of Works, Mr. Samuel Preston. The estimated cost, including swimming bath, furniture, and janitor's house, but exclusive of site, was £17,663 . . .

EVENING TIMES 16 *February* 1894.

PERSONALITIES

A great city like Glasgow has naturally attracted many interesting and important people. Some came in their youth to take part in its commercial and industrial enterprise, and are remembered as powerful and influential figures in the great days of the city's development. Unfortunately the majority of them were far too busy to have time for private idiosyncrasy, so their life stories tend to be more statistical than one would wish. The 18th century threw up a number of eccentrics who, although rich, were not allowed to enter the society of the real aristocrats, the Tobacco Lords or Virginia merchants. Robert McNair, grocer, merchant, and speculator, was one of them. His antics make one suspect the shrewd showmanship of a clever businessman. David Dale, the greatest of all the Glasgow merchants has been omitted here, but finds a place in another chapter. His commercial opposite, the miserly banker Robert Carrick, was naturally the butt of many tales, most of them probably true. He was one of a tiny minority who took everything they could from the city and gave back nothing in return. By contrast, the flamboyant figure of George Gordon with his fine team of horses, is typical of the many self-made men of the 19th century. He is a symbol of a less mechanised and more colourful age.

Although the great majority of foreign visitors to Britain seldom ventured further north than London, a few were foolhardy enough to make the effort. Of the great musicians, Paganini, Chopin, Liszt, and Mendelssohn came to Scotland. Chopin, in the last year of his short life, had been persuaded by a friend to come but, despite the kind attentions of the ladies of the county gentry, found the whole thing an ordeal. Other musical celebrities who came to the city are included, with some from the world of literature, the stage, the visual arts, and politics.

ROBERT McNAIR, THE ECCENTRIC GROCER

Mr. McNair was a man of abilities, but of very eccentric manners. Amongst his other whims, he ordered the key-stones of the arches above the shops in his building to be cut so as to represent ludicrous human faces, and each one to be different from another. It was a source of amusement to him, on market days, to join the crowds of country folks who were gazing upon these heads, and to hear their remarks upon them.

Many amusing anecdotes are told of Mr. McNair. At the time in question *(mid 18th century)* there were few individuals in Glasgow possessed of large capital; in consequence of which, all extensive undertakings were carried on there by joint-stock companies, having several partners, perhaps six or eight, who each respectively furnished his quota of capital. Such were our east and west Sugarhouse Companies, Tanwork Company, Soapwork Company, ... Ropework Company, Bottlework Company, ... and many others. Mr. McNair was resolved not to be behind these companies, and accordingly assumed his wife as a partner, and had his firm painted above his shop door, *Robert McNair, Jean Holmes, & Co.*

There happened one season to be rather a scarcity of oranges in Glasgow, and, unfortunately for Mr. McNair, his stock of them was very small, while a neighbouring grocer held nearly the whole stock of oranges in Glasgow. Mr. McNair, however, told all his customers that he had a large cargo of oranges, which he expected to arrive every hour. In the meantime, he made up apparently a barrow-load of oranges with his small stock, and employed a porter to wheel them past his neighbour grocer's shop, and to deliver them to his own shop (as if he was getting delivery of a cargo), but immediately afterwards he privately sent away the porter, with his load well covered, by a back door, and through cross streets, and made him again wheel the same barrowful of oranges (openly exposed) past his opponent's shop; and so the porter continued employed for many hours. Having thus apparently laid in a large stock of oranges, he engaged a person to call upon his neighbour grocer, and to buy his whole stock, which his friend did on very moderate terms, the grocer believing that Mr. McNair had received a large supply, and that certainly oranges would fall in value.

Mr. McNair kept his phaeton *(carriage)*, and had his town and country house. The latter was situated on the Camlachie Road, and he named this property "Jeanfield," after his wife, Jean Holmes. The house stood upon an eminence in the middle of a park of considerable extent, and it now forms the Eastern Cemetery. At this period Government laid on a tax upon two-wheeled carriages, to the great annoyance of Mr. McNair, who was determined to resist payment of this obnoxious tax, and therefore he took off the wheels from his phaeton, and placed the body of it upon two long wooden trams, on which machine he continued to visit his country house, and to carry Jean Holmes and his daughters to church.

The public of Scotland is indebted to Mr. McNair for obtaining the abolition of a shameful custom, which then existed in our

Exchequer Court. It was at that time the practice, in all Exchequer trials, for the Crown, when successful, to pay each juryman one guinea, and to give the whole of them their supper. It happened that Mr. McNair had got into some scrape with the Excise and an action was raised against him in the Exchequer Court at Edinburgh. When the case came to be called, the Crown Advocate, after narrating all the facts and commenting on them, concluded his address to the jury by reminding them, that if they brought in a verdict for the Crown, they would receive a guinea each, and their supper. Upon hearing which, Mr. McNair rose up, and asked the Judges if he might be allowed the liberty of speaking one word to the jury. To which request the Judges readily assented. Mr. McNair then turned round to the jury and thus addressed them:— "Gentlemen of the Jury, you have heard what the learned Advocate for the Crown has said, namely — 'that he will give you a guinea each, and your supper, if you bring in a verdict in favour of the Crown.' Now, here am I, Robert McNair, merchant in Glasgow, standing before you, and *I* promise you two guineas each, and your dinner to boot, with as much wine as you can drink, if you bring in a verdict in my favour;" and here Mr. McNair sat down. The trial went on, and Mr. McNair obtained a verdict in his favour. After this trial the Crown never made any attempt at influencing the jury by this species of bribery.

Mr. McNair had two daughters, buxom lasses, and, as he was known to be wealthy, these ladies had abundance of wooers; but Mr. McNair became afraid that they might make foolish marriages with some penniless young fellows; to prevent which, he inserted an advertisement in the newspapers, giving notice to all young men who might come a courting of his daughters that, unless his daughters married with his express consent and approbation, he would not give them one shilling of his property; and he requested all young men who might be looking after his daughters to attend to this notice.

GLASGOW PAST AND PRESENT *vol. 1 page 293.*

———————— * ————————

ROBERT CARRICK, THE MISER

... Mr. Carrick was the son, we think, of a clergyman in Renfrewshire, "passing rich on £80 a-year". He came into Glasgow a comparatively poor boy in early life, but he established, or at all events he became the chief or leading partner of, the old Ship Bank of Glasgow. ...

Robin Carrick, for that was the name he was always called in our recollection, amassed an immense fortune, nearly a million sterling; but he was one of the greatest *scrubs* or misers in relation to money matters, that Glasgow ever saw. He died, a grim old batchelor forty years ago, without leaving one plack or penny to any of the charitable institutions of the city, in which city he had derived the greater part of his enormous wealth. . . .

Mr. Carrick's housekeeper, viz., Miss Paisley, an elderly damsel, was also his favourite niece. They lived in the *upper flat* of the Bank premises, then at the corner of Glassford Street, whereon some spacious modern premises are now reared. The Bank itself was a dark dingy place; but a grand establishment of its kind in Glasgow sixty years ago; and while Mr. Carrick was famed for his vast banking transactions in the flat below, Miss Paisley was notorious throughout the city for the most niggardly management of his household in the flat above. She would *prig*, or higgle, or banter with the shopkeepers in King Street, then the chief provision place in the city, but now so deplorably deserted; she would try to beat them down to the value of a farthing about the price of beef, mutton, or veal. We have frequently seen her hurrying from the markets in King Street, with a sheep's-head and trotters in her basket, and a string of flounders or caller herring in her hands; and when she went to the higher station of markets in the Candleriggs, she invariably stipulated with the green-grocers in that place, that if any apples or pears should be left over at the contemplated dinner dessert of Mr. Carrick's table, they would just be taken back on the following morning to the place from whence they came, and paid for accordingly. No wonder the old miser and his amazon amassed riches to an almost incredible degree, by this miserable mode of living, so unworthy of persons of the most ample means. . . .

On one particular occasion, the old fellow, Robert Carrick, Esq., was waited upon by a deputation of two or three respectable citizens for his subscription to the Royal Infirmary, then in its infancy, or of some other institution of pressing importance. They expected that he being the wealthiest banker at the time in all the city, and knowing the urgent circumstances of the case, would head the list of subscribers with a pretty handsome donation. To their mortification and surprise, he would only come down with "Two Guineas". When they respectfully beseeched him to give something more, he waxed wroth, and was for drawing back his miserable pittance, but recollecting himself for a moment, he stated that he really could not *afford* to give them any more; and he literally bowed them out of his miserly room, encased as it was, with millions of money in the shape of bills or other documents.

Not far from that bank was the warehouse of old Mr. John McIlquham. . . . Mr. McIlquham was then doing a good stroke of business in the tambouring and manufacturing line in Glasgow. When the deputation, who had just left Banker Carrick, approached

Mr. McIlquham, he put on his spectacles, and glanced at the list of subscribers. He mused and commented on the trifling subscription of Mr. Carrick. "Bless me!" he said, "has he only given you '*Twa guineas*' for such a benevolent purpose?" "Not more," they replied; and they made this statement to the old plodding but liberal manufacturer. "Do you know," said they to Mr. McIlquham, "when we pressed him for more, he sulkily told us that he could not afford to give any more." "What's that you say?" and they repeated the words, very much apparently to his astonishment and ire. He rose from his three-legged stool with some animation. "Jamie!" said he to his faithful cash-keeper and confidant . . . — "Jamie! bring me the Ship Bank-book, and a cheque, and the ink-bottle, and a pen;" and with these materials before him, Mr. McIlquham filled up with his own hand a cheque on the Ship Bank for £10,000, or a much larger sum, as we have heard it stated to be. But no matter what the amount. It was a large one, certainly. "Now, Jamie, run down as fast as your legs can carry you to the Bank, and take care and be sure and bring that money to me, and the gentlemen of the deputation here will just kindly wait till you return." Of course, they agreed to do so, not knowing at that moment about the impending circumstance.

The cheque was presented at the Bank table, and a queer place it was. Old Robin stared, and he looked at it over and over again. "Go back," said he, "young man, to Mr. McIlquham, with my compliments, and tell him he has committed some *mistake*." "What!" said the old indignant manufacturer, when that message was communicated to him, "will Banker Carrick not give me my own money . . . so go back instantly, and tell Mr. Carrick from me, that there is no mistake whatsomever, on my part. The gentlemen here are still waiting, so *demand* the money in big notes." On this fresh, but imperative message, Mr. Carrick got rather *shakey* in his chair, and alarmed. There had been an understanding between him and his excellent customer, that when an unusual large supply of money was wanted from the Bank, a day or two's previous notice should be given, in order, as Robin remarked, that the wheels of the Bank might run on smoothly. So Mr. Carrick felt it now necessary to rise from his imperious seat, and to *steek* the door of his sanctum, . . . and to trudge away over, musing unto himself, to the capacious warehouse of Mr. McIlquham. "What's wrong wi' ye the day?" said the Banker, as he now saluted his customer. "Wrong with me!" said Mr. McIlquham, "Nothing in the least degree wrong wi' me, praise be blest! but I am dumfoundered, and suspect that there's surely something very far wrong with yourself and the Bank; for my friends, these douce decent gentlemen, sitting *ben* yonder, have assured me, that in your own premises, and out of your own mouth, you declared you could only afford to give them scrimp 'Twa guineas' for this praiseworthy purpose; and if that be the case, I think it is high time that I should remove some of my deposits out of your hands." This led to a most agreeable result. Robin, with some reluctance — but he did it — scribbled down his name to the subscription paper, at the request of Mr. McIlquham, for the sum of *Fifty guineas*; and Mr. McIlquham on that, cancelled his cheque for the £10,000, and the gentlemen of the deputation went away amazed, and perfectly delighted with this reception.

REMINISCENCES OF GLASGOW *Peter Mackenzie 1865 vol. I page 311.*

———————— * ————————

THE DEMON FIDDLER

THEATRE ROYAL

PAGANINI

SIGNOR PAGANINI respectfully announces to the Nobility Gentry, and Public resident in Glasgow and its vicinity, that he will give a

GRAND CONCERT

At the THEATRE, on MONDAY Evening, 23rd inst.

Being positively the Last Time he can possibly have the honour of appearing before them, previous to his departure for the Court of St. Petersburgh; on which occasion he has engaged those highly celebrated Vocalists

MISS WELLS AND MISS WATSON

The Concert will be arranged by MR. WATSON, Composer to the Theatres Royal, English Opera House and Covent Garden, and Member of the Royal Academy of Music.

Mr. Watson will preside at the Piano Forte.

BOXES, 7s 6d. — PIT, 5s. — GALLERY, 2s 6d.

GLASGOW HERALD *20 September 1833.*

SIGNOR PAGANINI, grateful for the liberal patronage he has experienced, respectfully announces to the Nobility, Gentry and Public, resident in Glasgow and its vicinity, that he will give his

FAREWELL CONCERT

And in order to afford an opportunity to all classes who may be desirous of hearing him, the *Prices of Admission will be reduced* as follows:—

BOXES, 6s. — PIT, 3s 6d. — GALLERY, 2s.

GLASGOW HERALD *27 September 1833.*

GREAT MUSICAL ATTRACTION
ASSEMBLY ROOMS, INGRAM STREET.

Mons. LISZT has the honour to announce to the Nobility and Gentry of Glasgow and its vicinity, that he intends giving

Two Grand
CONCERTS of VOCAL
and INSTRUMENTAL MUSIC,

The first to take place on MONDAY MORNING, January 18th, commencing at One o'clock, and the second on WEDNESDAY EVENING, the 20th. On which occasion Mons. LISZT will perform his Unrivalled Recitals, assisted by MISS STEELE, MISS LOUISA BASSANO, Mr. JOHN PARRY, Jun. (the celebrated Vocalists,) and Mr. RICHARDSON, (the eminent Flute Player).

CONDUCTOR — Mr. LAVENU

Tickets, Six Shillings each; Family Tickets, admitting Four, One Guinea. To be had at Mr. Mitchison's Music Saloon, 28, Buchanan Street, and at the principal Music Warehouses. *Reserved Seats, Seven Shillings each. To be had of Mr. Mitchison.*

GLASGOW HERALD *11 January 1841.*

THEATRE ROYAL, DUNLOP STREET.

On Tuesday evening this elegant theatre was filled with one of the most brilliant audiences that ever met within its walls. The occasion was one of more than ordinary attraction. In the first place the performance was given for the purpose of endowing a perpetual curatorship of Shakespere's House at Stratford. And next it was meant to insure, if possible, the appointment of Mr. Sheridan Knowles, who was for a large portion of his life a citizen of, and who wrote some of his earliest dramas in, Glasgow. And lastly, the Amateur Company was composed of persons who had rendered themselves eminent in literature and art. . . .

The pieces selected for the evening, were Shakespere's "Merry Wives of Windsor", and Mrs. Inchbald's "Animal Magnetism". It is needless to speak at any great length of these dramatic works. The first everyone knows, and of the second it is enough to say that it is a genuine farce, full of fun, racy dialogue, and good stage situations. We must confess to a certain hesitation and unwillingness to speak further of the performance, or to particularize when all was so worthy of praise. Nevertheless, we cannot choose but to express our opinion freely. We must give the first place to Mr. Dickens, whose *Slender* was finely conceived and given with a degree of half-witted hesitation and bashfulness which was quite delightful. He had evidently studied the part with great care, and he spoke and looked the very lover of "Sweet Anne Page" that Shakespere drew. . . .

In the after-piece Mr. Dickens sustained the character of the *Doctor*, and Mr. George Cruikshank that of his active and passive servant *Jeffrey*, in a manner that called down the most rapturous applause from all parts of the house. . . . At the close of the play, the audience joined in a round of unanimous and hearty applause, whereupon the curtain was drawn up and showed the party as at the finale. Mr. Dickens then stepped forward and announced that they would again perform on Thursday (last night), when the pieces would be "Used up", "Love, Law and Physic", and "Past Two o'clock in the Morning". Half the profits to be devoted to the aid of the unemployed of Glasgow. . . .

GLASGOW HERALD *21 July 1848.*

JENNY LIND IN OPERA
THEATRE ROYAL, DUNLOP STREET.

MADEMOISELLE JENNY LIND will appear in the
celebrated Opera of
LA FIGLIA DEL REGGIMENTO,
Supported by the great Tenor, M. ROGER, and the whole of the
COMPANY OF HER MAJESTY'S THEATRE,
ON MONDAY, OCTOBER 2nd,
And in the Opera of LA SONNAMBULA, on
WEDNESDAY THE 4th OCTOBER.

The Box Office will be open for the issue of Box and Pit Tickets only, on Tuesday the 29th instant, at Twelve o'clock: and on Wednesday, at the same hour, for the issue of Tickets to all other parts of the Theatre.

Prices are arranged as under:—

Lower Boxes, Dress Circle..25s.
Upper Boxes, Sides...10s 6d.
Upper Boxes, Stalls...15s.
Pit...21s.
Lower Gallery...5s.
Upper Gallery...3s.

Bills of the Performance, with a List of the splendid Band, may be had at the Music Shops, on Saturday and Monday, 26th and 28th instant.

GLASGOW HERALD 25 August 1848.

On Wednesday the Theatre Royal, Dunlop Street, which is itself one of the most compact and richly adorned theatres to be found anywhere, opened its doors to admit a fashionable and enthusiastic crowd of the admirers of the divine Jenny. The curtain rose to a few bars of exquisitely performed instrumental music, and the piece commenced. The first and second scenes were got over, and in the third scene, Jenny Lind, dressed like a good-natured rustic beauty, came upon the stage. The opening recitative was finely delivered, but the audience knew that her first song was in this scene, and were held in silent suspense waiting for the "Come per me sereno," which she sang with exquisite feeling. . . . Each new scene in which she appeared was remarkable for the peculiar graces of action and evidence of taste, education, and genius which she threw into them. Her performance was, so to speak, cumulative. It increased in interest, had added manifestations of musical skill and vocal execution in every scene. Up to the last cadenza of the closing scene, we know not that she had exhausted the resources of her wonderfully fertile musical imagination.

At the close of the finale . . . she was hailed for her triumphant song of joy with a round of applause, an encore was as unanimously called for, to which she bowed a smiling assent, and sung over the last movement with added brilliancy. What struck us particularly was the closing cadences of this fine bravura song. They were all wonderfully difficult and executed with the utmost ease, and sweetness of intonation. These were no mere exercises in scholastic scales, but grand vocal studies. The piano forte under the hands of Monsieur Chopin could alone work such musical miracles. The audience evidently felt this, for their enraptured plaudits rose in just proportion with the climax of art and voice, achieved by the Swedish girl. A cloud of bouquets covered the stage in compliment to her, and as she retired bowing, she sweetly and good-naturedly laughed as they fell upon and around her. . . .

The public are delighted with Jenny Lind, and would willingly pay a good sum for the pleasure of hearing her frequently, but lovers of good music in the country ought not to be mulcted out of their money under the pretext of her great reputation. The plain fact of the case is, that rapacious speculators make a trade of her divine gifts. They use her name to make fortunes in a week.

GLASGOW HERALD 9 *October 1848.*

M. CHOPIN'S CONCERT

On Wednesday, M. Chopin, the great French pianist gave a *matinee musicale* in the Merchants' Hall, under the patronage of the most distinguished ladies of the nobility and gentry of the West of Scotland. At half past two P.M., when the concert was to commence, a large concourse of carriages began to draw up in Hutcheson Street and the streets adjoining. The audience, which was not large, was exceedingly distinguished. Of M. Chopin's performance, and of the style of his compositions it is not easy to speak so as to be intelligible to unscientific musicians. His style is unique, and his compositions are very frequently unintelligible from the strange and novel harmonies he introduces. In the pieces he gave on Wednesday, we were particularly struck with the eccentric and original manner in which he chose to adorn the subject. He frequently took for a theme a few notes which were little else than the common notes of the scale. Those who were present at the entertainment would observe this in the *Nocturnes et Berceuse*. This simple theme ran through the whole piece, and he heaped on it the strangest series of harmonies, discords and modulations that can well be imagined. Again, in another subject, one single note of the key was heard with the monotonous pulsations moving through just as peculiar a series of musical embellishments.

One thing must have been apparent to every one of the audience, namely, the melancholy and plaintive sentiment that pervaded his music. Indeed, if we would choose to characterize his pieces in three words, we would call them novel, pathetic and difficult to be understood. M. Chopin is evidently a man of weak constitution and seems labouring under physical debility and ill health. Perhaps his constitutional delicacy may account for the fact that his musical compositions have all that melancholy sentiment which we have spoken of.

We incline to the belief that the master's compositions will always have a greater charm when heard *en famille* than in the concert room; at the same time we know that they possess certain technical peculiarities which must render them sealed treasures to by far the greatest number of amateur piano-forte performers. . . .

GLASGOW HERALD 29 *September 1848.*

A LIFE WITH HORSES

In our obituary yesterday many of our readers would observe with regret the death on the evening of Saturday last, at Cornton, Bridge of Allan, of Mr. George Gordon, railway contractor, late of Dockneyfaulds farm, Glasgow. Mr. Gordon from his early days had always a fondness for horses, and while yet a youth he completed a satisfactory engagement in the north of England as mail coach driver. Returning to Scotland, he, for many years acted as driver of the mail coaches which ran between Glasgow, Mearns and Eaglesham, the vehicles running on alternate days. He subsequently, after renting the farm of Netherlee at Cathcart, which he worked successfully; removed to Dockneyfaulds (*Cathcart Road near Caledonia Road*), where he remained until he retired from the business of railway contractor (which he had commenced after leaving the "coaching" work), a branch of service which he conducted with an energy and zeal which made his name almost a "household word" in railway and commercial circles.

Mr. Gordon, in the course of his career, made many friends among the nobility and gentry throughout the south and south-west of Scotland, and north of England. His company was much sought after by hosts of friends and acquaintances, who passed many a pleasant hour in listening to his enjoyable reminiscences of life on "the box". He was contractor for the West Highland mails for many years, and in a word, we may say his contracts were always fulfilled to the letter.

In 1848, when the Queen's Own Royal Regiment of Glasgow Yeomen Cavalry was started, Mr. Gordon, not then a youth, was amongst the first to come forward to join the regiment, and as an old stager remarked to us yesterday, "George always came out splendidly mounted, and could show some of his juniors how to sit in the saddle." The last time Mr. Gordon handled "the ribbons", four in hand, was on the occasion of the Volunteer Review in Edinburgh. Mr. Gordon then came out in style, dressed in his scarlet coat, buckskins, and light beaver, and surprised not a few as he drove down the Gallowgate with his happy party, as if he had been a younger man by thirty years. Some six or seven years ago, after a long life of hard labour and honest industry, Mr. Gordon gave up business, and retired to Cornton, Bridge of Allan, where he spent the remainder of his days in quietness. . . .

GLASGOW HERALD *14 January 1879.*

THE GREATEST ACTOR OF HIS AGE

If there were brave men before Agamemnon, so there have been popular actors before Mr. Irving; but I think it doubtful if there ever was an actor who created the same interest among that large class who are not habitual play-goers. There seems to be something magnetic about his personality which has an attraction even for people who take little note of theatrical doings. . . .

After the banquet given to Mr. Irving in London recently, presided over by Chief-Justice Coleridge, and attended by men of the highest position in every walk of life, any marks of admiration Mr. Irving may receive cannot surprise him. Nay, if he is at all cynically-minded he must at times be inclined to smile a little grimly at the flattery that is absolutely poured over him.

The guest of honour —
Henry Irving at the Pen and Pencil Club in 1883.

There is a sense, however, in which the banquet given to him by the Pen and Pencil Club, in the Art Institute, last Thursday, is a more remarkable proof of general esteem than even the great London one. We Northerners are confessedly less enthusiastic than our brethren of the sunny South, and more chary of expressing our feelings. When we begin to wave handkerchiefs and cheer ourselves hoarse in praise of any man, it may be taken for granted that he is really worthy of it. . . .

To simple-minded folks like myself, it is a never-ending source of surprise to find that a great man can eat his dinner, smoke a cigar, smile, walk about a room, shake hands, and chat pleasantly, just like less gifted mortals. To see a genius do all these things as if he enjoyed them is sufficient to tone down the awe with which I regard him into a respectful admiration. I will venture to say that there wasn't a man in the Institute on Thursday night who enjoyed the entertainment more than Mr. Irving did, if appearances can be believed.

QUIZ 14 September 1883.

————————— * —————————

THE APOSTLE OF THE BEAUTIFUL

No characteristic of our time is more marked than that which reserves eminence in any walk of life for the middle-aged and the old. It is no longer possible to be a Prime Minister or an artist of world-wide fame at five-and-twenty, and a politician or a man of science at fifty is looked on as one who has his career still before him. The world is too old and hardened to be readily conquered by the enthusiasm of youth.

To this state of matters Mr. Oscar Wilde, who at twenty-eight finds himself one of the best-known men in Britain, is a singular exception. No doubt the stars in their courses have fought for his popularity, and possibly he owes his present position less to anything he himself has said or done than to what has been said and done about him by some of the most brilliant wits of the day. The ridicule heaped on the aesthetic movement and its leader . . . has had much the same effect that persecution and martyrdom have had on religious belief; and the more Mr. Wilde was caricatured, the wider grew his circle of sympathetic followers.

The new cult has been represented as a mixture of hypocrisy and downright silliness, but had it consisted entirely of lily-worship and grovelling before Botticelli it would have been dead in six months. The truth is that a living and life-giving principle underlay the eccentricities of the movement. The love of beauty for its own sake, apart from any utilitarian object, the sense of the loveliness of

[49]

common things, and the desirableness of harmonious domestic surroundings — these were revelations of which the present generation stood much in need, and for them we have to thank Mr. Wilde and his fellow-prophets. . . .

Apart from his position as apostle of the beautiful, Mr. Wilde is a man of wide and brilliant attainments. Born at Dublin in 1855, the son of the eminent oculist Sir William Wilde, he enjoyed all the advantages of the most refined home training and example. In 1874

Oscar Wilde after a lecture in St Andrew's Halls in 1883.

he entered Magdalen College, Oxford, where he distinguished himself by taking two first-classes, as well as by gaining the Newdigate prize by his poem, "Ravenna". During his residence at Oxford he was a copious contributor of verses to various magazines, and in 1881 his first volume of poems was published. Since then he has devoted himself to lecturing, first in America, and more recently in this country.

With a tall, handsome, heavy-built figure, a manner of languid frankness, and an almost too persistent smile, Mr. Wilde's influence has been exerted personally rather than through literary channels. He has outgrown those absurdities of dress and manner that were sport for the Philistines in his early youth, and no one can listen to him for five minutes without being impressed by his cool common-sense, his shrewd humour, and his natural eloquence. Emphatically, he is a man with a future.

QUIZ *14 December 1883.*

———————— * ————————

The third lecture of the Sunday Society series was delivered by Mr. Oscar Wilde in St. Andrew's Halls last evening, the subject being "Artistic *v* Modern Dress". The hall was filled. He said there had been developed within the last few years in this country an artistic taste and a revival of artistic feeling that was without parallel in the history of any art of this century. It was impossible to go into any house without seeing at once that a very great change was taking place. There was a far greater feeling for colour, a far greater feeling for the delicacy of form, and a sense that art can touch the very commonest things of a household into a certain grace and loveliness. Dress was an art, and without exaggerating its importance he believed that to dress well one should be a master of colour and form. Dress, in the first place, should be expressive of the beauty and proportions of that which it covered, and not, as it so often happened, merely a highly-decorated prison that confined and limited the freedom of the body under it. The beauty of dress depended on its expressing properly the human form. If a child were taught to draw the outline of the human figure it would soon learn that the waist is a very delicate and beautiful curve, and not, as the dressmaker fondly imagines, an abrupt right angle suddenly occurring in the centre of the person. (Laughter.)

All art was the expression of certain laws and principles, which remained the same whether one was decorating a room or designing a dress. In speaking of artistic colour, he remarked that all colours were good and equally beautiful, and were to the decorative artist what the notes of a piano were to the musician. One note was not

lovelier than another, nor one colour ever more beautiful than its neighbour. Certain combinations of colour were good, and it was with the combination always that art, whether of music or decoration had to do. Nothing distressed him more than to see in a paragraph that such and such a colour was going to be very fashionable next season, and he held that it would not be more ridiculous to read in a musical magazine that B flat was going to be a very fashionable note next season. (Laughter.) ... Speaking generally of the nineteenth century, he said all the beautiful things had been made when something useful was attempted, and all the ugly things when something beautiful was tried. (Applause.)
GLASGOW HERALD *22 December 1884.*

---

*

THE PIONEER ARTIST-SOCIALIST

It is well that leaders of thought in any department of political or other affairs should learn a lesson which has been borne in upon Mr. William Morris, the Poet-Socialist. I have just been reading a letter of his in which he says:— "It seems to me that the Scotch are much given to 'lion-hunting', and that, therefore, it is necessary for a Socialist who wants to get at the facts, to discount a certain amount of enthusiasm with which he is received, if he happens to have any reputation outside Socialism." On coming north for the first time, the author of "The Earthly Paradise" modestly attributed the cordial reception given him not to appreciation of his personal qualities, but to sympathy with his efforts to "spread the light." It appears to me, from the tone of this epistle, that he is now well-nigh disillusioned, although, doubtless, he will be about the last man to make the admission.
QUIZ *9 July 1886.*

READINGS BY MR. WILLIAM MORRIS

Last night Mr. William Morris, author of "The Earthly Paradise", gave a series of readings from his own works before a select audience in the Queen's Rooms. Professor Nichol presided. In opening the proceedings he said he hoped there were comparatively few present who required to be introduced, in a sense, in reality, to one of the most thoroughly original poets of our time. . . . The peculiarity, and he thought the excellence of Mr. Morris was that he was a great deal more than a poet. He was a man of action, experience, and philanthropy; and whether they agreed with him or not on his projects they must all sympathise with him in the great movements that tended to advance the happiness of all classes of society. . . .

The audience listened to Mr. Morris with marked attention, and very warmly applauded his efforts. Mr. Morris, in replying to a vote of thanks at the close, said that in writing his poems he had had a most intense pleasure in the work itself. He thought the audience would probably agree with him, at all events, whatever they might think about other *dicta* he put forward, that one of the main objects — almost the main object — of human life as it is today was, that people should have work which was both pleasant to do and worthy of the doing. That was really the chief end aim of civilisation, unless it was becoming a mere empty name. He could only say further, whatever views he put forward he most sincerely held them, and he was willing to spend his life and time in furthering them so far as that went. Never in any circumstances — in no circumstances whatever — would he consent to a world without art. That he hoped was perfectly and thoroughly understood. The mere utilitarianism which some people had preached was a thing to be rejected, he would not say by all men of feeling, but by all men of sense, all men who knew what life is, that we must all agree to. He would say in favour of the line of thought and action he had taken up, that it would breed art, higher and better art than any we had yet had, through, it might be, an immense amount of tribulation and discouragement.

GLASGOW HERALD 25 April 1885.

———————— * ————————

NATIVE TALENT

No pianist, excepting Rubinstein (*Anton*), has ever attracted so great an assemblage in Scotland as did Mr. Fred. Lamond at his second recital, in St. Andrew's Hall on Friday last — the audience filling the great hall in every part. The programme opened with Tausig's arrangement of Bach's Toccata and Fugue in D minor, which received every justice at the pianist's hands. The succeeding piece, Beethoven's Sonata (Op. 57) in F minor, also was cleverly manipulated, *morendo* passages notably being given with consummate skill. As regards the reading of the opening movement, however, considerable caprice in the *tempo* was shown by the pianist, who kept continually varying it. . . .

In a Ballade, Mazurka, Nocturne, and Fantaisie, by Chopin, following, the performer was thoroughly in his element, and gave them all with infinite grace and poetical expression. He was equally at home in Schumann's Fantaisie (Op. 17), and evinced a degree of ideality, whilst playing it, surprising at his years. . . . At the conclusion the soloist received a well deserved ovation, and also a laurel wreath. The latter, however, most thoughtful people must have judged a very injudicious tribute. Laurels are not for those on the threshold of a career, however fair they may promise, but rather for those who have concluded the fight, or, at least, have sustained it a long time.

QUIZ 26 March 1886.

---------------- * ----------------

THE GRAND OLD MAN

I suppose it is merely a common-place to say that Mr. Gladstone seems periodically to renew his youth. It is at any rate beyond dispute that he looks very much more vigorous now than he did last winter. The appearances he made in the Music Hall, Edinburgh, on Friday and Monday, and in Hengler's Cirque on Tuesday, were

Gladstone lecturing by candlelight in Hengler's Circus.

really marvellous. I missed something of the silvery quality which characterised his voice of old, but still it was highly musical. The constant play of expression on his face and the accompanying gestures have to be seen to be fully realised. Twym (A. S. Boyd), who made sketches on one of the occasions referred to, has, however, done much to convey some impression of these to the vast majority of people who were deprived of the opportunity of witnessing them. The arrangements in Edinburgh were very much better than those in Glasgow, for it almost seemed for a time as though the meeting at the latter city would have to be abandoned. Of the numerous incidents in the Cirque, perhaps the most amusing was supplied by Mr. Gilbert Beith, M.P., who struck a match to enable the Premier to read a quotation. The cry was at once raised for candles, and these continued to be brought on to the platform long after the quotation had been finished.

QUIZ 25 June 1886.

--------------------------- * ---------------------------

A FEW STINGS IN THE TAIL

The treatment of the poor should be characterised by neither the evangelical frenzy of General Booth, the founder of the Salvation Army, nor the economical fantasy of Wm. Morris, the author of "The Earthly Paradise", two personages who have been in the city this week. On the afternoon of Monday the General arrived at Queen Street Station, accompanied by "foreign representatives from nearly all parts of the world," and indulged in "triumphant marches" through the city, followed by meetings of the usual kind. William Morris was engaged on the same day preaching the doctrines of Socialism, with which he has, to the regret of many who admire his character and his works, identified himself.

I have no doubt that in both cases the men are doing what they regard as good work among the poor, but their efforts are, in many instances, producing results which are to be deeply regretted.

QUIZ 2 July 1886.

Mr. Walter Crane, who lectured last night on the educational value of art, in the Waterloo Rooms, is tall and straight, and a bad lecturer. His style is too jerky. "Friend Crane," said the author of "The Earthly Paradise," is both true artist and true Socialist.

EVENING TIMES 4 November 1889.

WEATHER

What can one say about Glasgow's weather except that it is invariably dreadful? It takes something quite outrageous to reach the headlines so reports tend to be few and far between. The terrible famine years of the 1690s and early 1700s did not affect the towns in the same way that they did the countryside where people were often driven to desperation. Apart from the occasional freak storm the worst danger in the city was from flooding from the undeepened river. This danger was removed with the river improvements including miles of quays and embankments, in the 19th century. The long frost of the winter 1784-5 with the river frozen over, seems to have been seized upon as an occasion for unwonted high jinks.

* * *

AN EARLY FROST

The provest, bailleis, and counsall, having knawledge and consideratioun that Ninian Andirsoun, deakin conveiner, did incur los . . . be vehement frost, quhairby the river of Clyd wes closit be the space of xvj oulkis (16 weeks), sua that na leadining (*loading*) of heirng could be at the said river during the said space, nor yit could cum to the brig of the said burghe, bot altogidder transportit be iis to sindrie pairtis of the cuntrie, . . . hes thairfoir remittit and dischargit to him (the sum of forty pounds).

EXTRACTS FROM THE BURGH RECORDS *17 September 1608*.

* * *

On Friday, betwixt the Hours of four and five Afternoon, a sudden Whirlwind carried about 200 Pieces of Table and Body Linen (which was drying in the Green) streight up in the Air, so high that many of them were out of Sight; and some of them, about 15 Minutes after, were seen falling above Half a Mile's Distance from the Place. The Evening's being calm, and no other Part touch'd, tho' there was plenty of Linen lying all round it, makes it appear the more surprising. We had this Account from several Gentlemen who were Eye-Witnesses.

GLASGOW JOURNAL *15 March 1742*.

The most memorable flood is that of Tuesday, 12th March 1782, which is still remembered by some living in the light of a "judgment". After long and heavy rains, the Clyde rose on the afternoon of Monday to an alarming extent. It covered all the lower parts of the Green, stopped the communication with the country to the south by the bridges, and laid the Bridgegate under water to the depth of several feet. As the inhabitants were accustomed to floods, many of them went to bed in the hope that the waters would have subsided by the morning; but they continued to rise during the night until the fires on the ground floors were extinguished, and then the flood entered the beds, from which the inmates hastily retreated to the upper storeys. The night was a wild, dark, and dismal one; there were heard throughout the whole street cries of distress and despair; and at the distance of more than half-a-century many of the Bridgegate denizens still spoke of it as the most gloomy night they had every spent in their lives. By early daylight the inhabitants were relieved by means of boats, which sailed up and down the street, supplying the families with cordials and provisions, and removing such of them as desired to escape from their dwellings. The lower parts of Saltmarket, Stockwell, and Jamaica Streets were in the same condition; and the then village of Gorbals was so completely surrounded that it seemed like an island rising up in the midst of an estuary. A young woman was drowned there, which was the only loss of life occasioned by the flood; but a great many horses and cows were drowned in their stables, and the merchants suffered much from vast quantitites of tobacco, sugar, and other merchandise having been carried away or damaged. The flood subsided in the course of Tuesday, and on Wednesday the Clyde returned to its wonted channel, after having at one time risen no less than twenty feet above its ordinary level.

GLASGOW PAST AND PRESENT *vol. I page 109.*

——————— * ———————

METEOR

On Monday the 18th of August, 1783, the meteor which had been the cause of general alarm, was seen at Glasgow at nine o'clock in the evening. Its appearance was that of a fiery ball, with a conical tail; and it moved in a direction from north-east to south-west with inconceivable velocity. Its light was so strong and brilliant, that a pin might have been picked up on the street; and, what is remarkable, it was seen over all Britain nearly at the same instant — a proof that its height must have been very great.

CHAPMAN'S PICTURE OF GLASGOW *1818 page 38.*

Sunday last about ten o'clock it began to snow, which continued all that day and night without intermission, attended with a high wind at east and north east. It lay very deep in the country, and obstructed the arrival of the post from London by Carlisle, till eight o'clock on Monday evening. The London post by Edinburgh did not arrive till six o'clock on Tuesday evening.

A woman who had been at church in this city, travelling home on Sunday evening, perished in the snow, about three miles north of this town, and within a quarter of a mile of her own door. Her body was found on Tuesday.

GLASGOW MERCURY *3 February 1785*.

---

*

On the 14th of March 1785, the ice on the Clyde broke up after four months frost; during this period, booths and dram shops, with fires in them, were erected on the River.

ABRIDGEMENT OF THE ANNALS OF GLASGOW
Cleland. 1817. page 41.

---

*

The beginning of this winter was remarkably mild, but since Christmas there has not been so severe a winter in Scotland, since the year 1740.

GLASGOW COURIER *31 January 1795*.

---

*

INTENSE FROST

As a singular proof, among others, of the intenseness of the frost, on Sunday morning last a crow was discovered frozen to death on a branch of a tree at the upper end of Frederick-street.

GLASGOW COURIER *7 February 1795*.

---

*

WINTER SEASON AT THE THEATRE

MR KEMBLE has the honour to inform the Ladies and Gentlemen of Glasgow, and the Public at large, that several persons are employed in clearing all the avenues leading to the Theatre; and that good fires are kept in every part of the House, to render it warm and comfortable.

GLASGOW COURIER *10 February 1795*.

ANOTHER FLOOD

On the 18th November 1795 the Clyde again "wide o'er the brim with many a torrent swelled"; and, as before, the lower parts of the city were completely submerged. About midday two of the arches of the bridge, then recently erected at the foot of Saltmarket, fell down with a crash, and the displacement of water was so tremendous that the doors of the public washing-house, though situated at a great distance, were burst open, and a portion of the clothes and utensils floated away. The remaining arches fell in the course of the afternoon, and thus the edifice was entirely destroyed. During this flood a boy was drowned in attempting to reach his home at the foot of the New Wynd.

GLASGOW PAST AND PRESENT *vol. I page 110.*

———————— * ————————

A DINNER PARTY SAVED

The familiar stocky figure of David Dale.

Amidst all these distressing occurrences there happened one so comic that its recital by the tittle-tattlers of the day made people almost to forget the general calamity caused by the flood. It seems that David Dale, Esq., whose house was situated at the foot of Charlotte Street, had invited a large party to dinner on the said 18th day of November 1795, and expected William Simpson, cashier of the Royal Bank, the great millionaire Gilbert Innes of Stowe, and the whole posse of the Royal Bank directory, to come from Edinburgh to meet Scott Moncrieff, George McIntosh, and a few others of our Glasgow magnates at dinner on the said day.

On the memorable morning of the said 18th, all was bustle and hurry-burry in Mr. Dale's house, preparing a sumptuous feast for this distinguished party. The kitchen fires were in full blaze, prompt to roast the jolly joints of meat already skewered on the spits, to boil the well-stuffed turkeys, and to stew the other tit-bits of the table;

while the puddings and the custards stood ready on the dresser for immediate application to the bars of the grate; when, lo and behold! the waters of the Clyde began gently to ooze through the chinks of the kitchen floor, and by-and-by gradually to increase, so that in a short time the servants came to be going through their work with the water above their ankles.

At this critical moment the Monkland canal burst its banks, and, like an avalanche, the waters came thundering down by the Molendinar Burn, carrying all before it, and filling the low houses of the Gallowgate, Saltmarket, Bridgegate, and under portions of St. Andrew's Square, with a muddy stream, and the wrecks of many a poor man's dwelling. In consequence of the regorgement of water caused by this sad mishap, and the continued increase of the flood, the Camlachie Burn, which ran close by Mr. Dale's house, was raised to an unusual height, and at once with a confused crash, broke into Mr. Dale's kitchen, putting out all the fires there, and making the servants to run for their lives, they having scarcely had time to save the half-dressed dinner.

Then came the great question — what was now to be done? The dinner hour was fast approaching, and the great Edinburgh visitors were already whirling rapidly towards Glasgow in their carriages; while the fires of the kitchen being completely extinguished, the kitchen itself was thereby rendered totally useless. In this calamitous dilemma, Mr. Dale applied to his opposite neighbour in Charlotte Street, William Wardlaw Esq., . . . for the loan of his kitchen, and also to another of his neighbours, Mr. Archibald Paterson, for a like accommodation, both of whom not only readily granted the use of their kitchens, but also the aid of their servants to cook Mr. Dale's dinner. But still the question remained — how were the wines, spirits, and ales to be gotten from the cellar, which now stood four feet deep of water? After much cogitation, a porter was hired, who, being suitably dressed for the occasion, was to descend to the abyss and bring up the said articles. It, however, occurred to Mr. Dale that the porter would not be able to distinguish the binns that contained the port, sherry, and Madeira (Mr. Dale did not sport French wines) from those of the rum, brandy, porter, and ale.

In this emergency, Miss Dale, then sixteen years of age, was mounted on the porter's back, and both having descended to the cellar, Miss Dale, amidst the waters of the deep, pointed out to her chevalier where he was to find the different articles required for the table. After having received instructions, the porter brought up his fair charge to the lobby of the house, where Miss Dale dismounted from the shoulders of her bearer in safety; and the porter having again descended to the cellar, readily found the wines and ales that were wanted, which he delivered to Mr. Dale in good order.

All things now went on in a satisfactory manner. The Edinburgh visitors and Glasgow magnates arrived in due time, the dinner was cooked and placed on the table in the best style, and the whole party passed the evening in mirth and jocularity at the odd circumstances which had attended this merry meeting.

GLASGOW PAST AND PRESENT *vol. III page 119.*

———————— * ————————

STORM DAMAGE

BY ORDER OF THE DEAN OF GUILD COURT

As, during the late stormy weather, a number of the CHIMNEY STACKS must have been damaged, and the CANS on the top of them loosened, which will occasion great danger upon a return of the like inclement weather — THE DEAN OF GUILD and his BRETHREN do hereby strictly enjoin and require all Proprietors of Houses within the City, without delay, to cause the Stacks of Chimneys of their Houses to be inspected by tradesmen, and such repairs as may be found necessary to be forthwith made, certifying such as neglect to comply with this order, that tradesmen will be appointed by the Court to inspect and do the necessary repairs at their expense.

GLASGOW HERALD *29 December 1806.*

Tuesday afternoon, between four and five o'clock, there was a violent storm of thunder and lightning in this City, accompanied with an extra ordinary fall of rain and hail. We do not recollect ever having seen such large and solid hailstones — a vast proportion of those which were regular, measured two inches in circumference; great numbers of pieces of ice of about two inches long, an inch broad, and fully half an inch thick, were found; in the centre of the mass, a regular formed hailstone was generally very obvious, and one piece fell into a court near the foot of Duke-Street, which measured five inches by four in circumference. The lightning was peculiarly vivid, while the rain was poured down in streams, that resembled more the awful visitations of warmer climates, than any thing that was ever experienced in this country. The sewers were insufficient to carry away the sudden inundation, which in many places extended from the sides to the centre of the streets, forming one sheet of water; and in some of the sunk shops and cellars, in the course of ten minutes after it began, the water was between 2 and 3 feet deep.

Innumerable panes of glass were broken over all the City and immediate neighbourhood, and the cupolas and skylights were in general drove in or much damaged; and we were witness to a considerable contusion that was produced by one of the hailstones, on the head of a young man who had gone out without his hat. This storm, we understand, was felt but a little distance from this City; and we have not heard of any serious accident having happened. The thunder broke near Partick, and knocked down part of a gateway.

GLASGOW HERALD *21 August 1807.*

———————— * ————————

In consequence of incessant heavy rain from nine o'clock on Saturday night, till eight o'clock on Sunday night, the River Clyde rose to a greater height than it has attained since the new bridge was carried off, nearly twelve years ago; and had it not been for the judicious mode of embanking lately adopted opposite to the Broomielaw, it is supposed that the water would in all probability have got to as great a height as it did on the memorable 12th March 1782. The whole of the Bridgegate was flooded last night, and continues so still; and the water has advanced a considerable way up Jamaica-Street, the Stockwell, and the Saltmarket. The bridges being inaccessible by foot passengers, carts are regularly plying at the foot of Jamaica-Street and Stockwell. — Two arches of the new bridge over the Clyde near Hamilton, on the road betwixt that Town and Edinburgh, fell, we are told, yesterday; and the damage done to the harvest on the low grounds along the river must have been very great, as large quantities of corns have floated past yesterday and today. A young man in a boat near the Clyde Iron-works, attempting to secure some of the floating grain, unfortunately lost his life.

GLASGOW HERALD *7 September 1807.*

———————— * ————————

Yesterday afternoon, we had a great deal of thunder and lightning, accompanied by excessively heavy rain. About a quarter past four, the lightning struck the top of Lord Nelson's Monument; and we regret to say that it has most materially injured that elegant structure. On the north side, the column is torn open for more than twenty feet from the top, and several of the stones have been thrown down. On the west side, the effects of the destructive fluid are visible in more than one place; and on the south side there is a rent in the column as far down as the head of the pedestal. A number of the stones are hanging in such a threatening posture, that a military guard has very properly been placed around the Monument, to keep at a distance the thoughtless or too daring spectators.

ROYAL INFIRMARY

Yesterday near two o'clock, while the Physicians were going their rounds, there was a violent thunder clap, without any perceptible interval between the flash and the stroke, which seemed to shake the Infirmary. All the chimnies were affected but particularly the western. The lowest of the women's wards, where the writer of this was, exhibited a very awful appearance. During four or six seconds all the flame was suddenly drawn into the ward with a rustling noise, together with a dense column of soot and smoke which instantly filled the ward. Fortunately no person was hurt; but the Patients screamed aloud, and such as could rise ran from their beds. Similar appearances, though in different degrees, took place through the whole house, which seems to have been enveloped in a thunder cloud, and which probably may have owed its preservation to the quantity of rain flowing from its roof. This occurrence, and the injury of Nelson's Monument, suggest the propriety of guarding every building, much exposed, by Thunder rods, which, when properly constructed, have never failed to prove a safe guard.

GLASGOW HERALD 6 *August 1810.*

Typical Glasgow Weather.

CHILDREN

The 17th and 18th century attitude to children was almost as callous as that towards animals. It was taken for granted that they would be useful to their parents, and that as early as possible. This attitude was probably responsible for the malicious pranks indulged in by Senex and his contemporaries although they belonged to the middle-class and might have been expected to know better. With the coming of the Industrial Revolution towards the end of the 18th century the plight of poorer children worsened considerably with their employment down coal mines and in cotton mills. It was their size of course which made them so useful in those places, and it was the same quality which fitted them for use (or rather misuse), as chimney sweeps. Legislation, as in so many other evil things, was slow to intervene, and it was not until 1842 that the use of boys for chimney-sweeping was made illegal. It is also surprising to see how long the strict servitude of apprenticeship was enforced — just imagine the outcry at anything like this today! The plight of the nine-year-old who ran away without shoes or stockings in the middle of winter tells us a great deal about contemporary attitudes. The vindictive advertisement placed by his master clearly tells us that his concern was not for the boy's welfare, but simply for the loss of work — and the new corduroy calshes! Of course, all masters were not like that, but it shows where the sympathies of the harsh legal system lay. What a change had taken place by the 1880s when civilisation seems to have replaced slavery, and the most important thing in life was the momentous decision which had to be made regarding the profitable spending of one's Saturday penny!!

---------------- * ----------------

PIGEON TROUBLE

In answer to Coline Campbell his desyre, in craving licence to build some little fixit work befoir his dowcat doir on the Greine, for withalding of boyes thairfrae wha troubles his dowes be chapping at all tymes on the said doire, the saids magistratis and counsell does heirby grant to the said Coline the said licence according to his said desyre.

EXTRACTS FROM THE BURGH RECORDS 6 *August* 1653.

WE Robert McNair and Jean Holmes, having taken into our consideration the way
and manner our daughter Jean acted in her marriage; that she took none of our advice, nor advised us before she married; for which reason we
discharged her from our family, for more than
twelve months: and being afraid that some or o-
ther of our family may also presume to marry
without duly advising us thereof; we, taking the
affair into our serious consideration, hereby discharge all and every one of our children from of-
fering to marry without our special advice and
consent first asked and obtained: and if any of
our children should propose or presume to offer
marriage to any, without, as aforesaid, our advice and consent; they, in that case are to be banished from our family twelve months; and if
they should go so far as to marry without our advice and consent, in that case they are to be banished from the family seven years: but whoever
advises us of their intention to marry, and ob-
tains our consent, shall not only remain children
of the family, but also shall have a due proportion of our goods, gear, and estate, as we shall
think convenient, and as the bargain requires:
and further, if any of our children shall marry
clandestinely they, by so doing, shall lose all
claim or title to our effects, goods, gear, or estate.
And we intimate this to all concerned, that none
may pretend ignorance.
EDINBURGH COURANT 28 October 1758.

———— * ————

18th CENTURY BYE-LAWS

That all boys shall be discharged by their parents and masters from
playing tops, shinty, or using any diversion whatever upon the flags
that may be incommodious to the inhabitants; they are likewise
discharged from playing shinty in the Green.

That all boys, or others, who shall be detected, at any time,
throwing stones, making bonfires, crying for illuminations, or

attempting to make any disturbance on the streets of this city, calculated to endanger the public peace, shall be punished with the utmost severity. On all such occasions parents and masters are to be accountable for their children or apprentices, and a reward is hereby offered of Five Pounds sterling to any person who shall detect or discover boys, or others, guilty of these practices, to be paid on conviction of the offenders.

That all parents and masters shall do their utmost to prevent their children and apprentices from going about in an idle manner on Sunday, and particularly from appearing in the streets or closes during Divine service, the magistrates being determined to punish all such offenders in the most exemplary manner.

GLASGOW MERCURY 22 March 1781 (GLASGOW PAST AND PRESENT vol. III page 194).

———————— * ————————

JUVENILE PRANKS

There was, however, another kind of battle, which still continued — I mean snow-ball battles — during the winter season. Many of these battles took place in the High Street, betwixt the collegians and grammar-school boys; but these were not fair battles; for the collegians being much older than their opponents, were sure to carry the day. There were, however, large parties of boys of tender age, who would form themselves into a phalanx in the public streets, and would order every passenger, high or low, to make obeisance to them on passing — the men to take off their hats, and the women to drop them a curtsey — and woe betide those who refused to obey; for in this case he or she was most unmercifully pelted with snow-balls. This sport was continued for many years by the little boys of Glasgow after stone battles had ceased; and remembering my having had a share in this sort of sport in my infantile days, I took good care, when grown up, upon passing one of these phalanxes, to take my hat off to them, and, in addition, I saluted them with a gracious smile and a most profound bow of respect, by which means I never failed to escape all molestation from the little gentlemen. But it was the country lads and lasses who gave these boys the most sport; for these rustics felt indignant at being peremptorily called upon to take off their hats, or to beck to a parcel of infants, and so refused to obey the order, upon which they were assailed with a perfect shower of snow-balls, and then were obliged either to take to their heels, or to pursue the little rascals, who, however, were seldom caught. . . .

One of the favourite places of our resort was at the gate of

Hutchesons' Hospital, which then stood at the foot of Hutcheson Street . . . This gate was made of strong timber for about four feet from the ground, and above that there were open spars, through which the inmates of the hospital could converse with anyone upon the street. This gate shut with a check, so that no person could get in to the hospital court from the outside unless the gate was opened by some one in the inside. Now upon the Wednesdays (which are our market days) we took possession of this gate, and watched carefully until we saw a countryman passing, with a fine walking-stick in his hand; one of us then immediately sallied forth, and getting slyly behind the rustic, whipped away his fine stick in a twinkling, and then ran within the hospital gate, which was directly *clinked to* by one of our confederate boys. The countryman, of course, pursued the delinquent, but here he was stopped by the impenetrable gate. We then, in a most provoking manner addressed him through the open spars, "Weel, John, hoo's a' wi' ye — hoo's the wife and the weans, man — are they a' brawly?" The countryman generally stormed and raged for the loss of his fine stick, but could find no means of getting at us, unless he ran round by the Candleriggs to the old Cow Loan, and scaled the hospital wall; but even then we had sufficient time to see him running down the hospital garden, and to open the gate, and scamper off. We often had compassion, however, upon a merry fellow, if he took up the joke in good humour, and spoke us fairly, and so restored him his stick through the spars; but we always took good care to see him surely away before we returned to open the gate.

Another of our tricks was to find out two houses upon the same stairhead, having their outer doors right opposite each other. These doors we quietly fastened at night to each other by strong ropes, and then we made the most thundering rap, rap, rap at each door, and, at the same time, called out, "Fire, fire, fire!" The poor inmates, in the greatest state of alarm, rushed to their respective doors, and then, when one pulled to get his door opened, his neighbour, who was as much frightened, pulled against him; and so they continued pulling and struggling together to get out, until some one, who lived at hand, hearing the uproar, came to their relief, and cut the ropes.
GLASGOW PAST AND PRESENT *vol. 1 page 286.*

AMISSING

JOHN MILLAR, Apprentice to Hepburn and Stewart, flax-dressers in Glasgow. He is of a fair complexion, 15 years old, and about five feet high, had on, when he went off, a round hat, a short red jacket, and white breeches.

As he has hitherto behaved to the satisfaction of his masters and friends, they are under the utmost anxiety for his welfare. If he returns he will be forgiven this fault.

If any persons employ him after this public notice, they will be prosecuted as the law directs.

His masters hereby offer Two Guineas of reward to any person who produces the said John Millar at their workshop, Bridgegate.

GLASGOW MERCURY 3 March 1785.

APPRENTICE RUN OFF

On Wednesday the 28th, ult. JOHN McCONNELL, apprentice to Jonathan Tomlinson, weaver, Calton, left his work. He is about nine years of age, four feet high, fair hair and fair complexion. Had on an old blue jacket and a pair of new corduroy calshes, but neither shoes, stockings nor hat.

Any person who will bring the said Boy to his Master, will receive HALF-A-GUINEA of Reward; and those who employ him after this intimation, will be prosecuted with the utmost rigour.

GLASGOW COURIER 15 December 1804.

RAN AWAY

From his Apprenticeship, on the 29th of May last, JOHN JACKSON, Stocking Maker, 16 years of age, brown hair, and squints with both eyes; had on when he went away, a brown jacket, yellow striped vest, and blue trowsers.

Whoever will give information where he may be found, to James Pickin, stocking maker, Clyde Street, Anderston, will receive ONE GUINEA of Reward, and their names concealed, if desired.

GLASGOW HERALD 16 June 1806.

———————— * ————————

CAUTION TO APPRENTICES

George Fyfe, apprentice moulder with Messrs, George Smith & Sons, Sun Foundry, was convicted of having deserted his employment, in breach of his indenture, and sentenced to thirty days imprisonment with hard labour.

GLASGOW HERALD 27 September 1864.

HEARTLESS THEFTS

Yesterday afternoon, while some children were diverting themselves in a closs in Trongate, a woman audaciously came up to a girl of about five years of age and stripped her of her frock, and made off with it, saying that she was going to bring her a new one. Same day, in Miller-Street, another child was almost stripped naked, even to her shoes.

GLASGOW COURIER 20 June 1800.

------------ * ------------

THE HAZARDS OF CHIMNEY SWEEPING

Wednesday an instance of very extraordinary cruelty on the part of a chimney-sweep towards a climbing-boy was exposed at the police court. The former, a lad upwards of 20, had been sent with a boy about nine years of age to clean a chimney in Graham (*now Bell*) Street; and he commenced the work by ordering the boy, and threatening him if he refused, to ascend the chimney, which one of the witnesses stated was only 9 inches wide. The boy was in tears, but notwithstanding the remonstrances of the women of the house, was compelled to climb, and the heartless monster who was tyrannising over him, reached up his brush and struck him on the feet, calling out at the same time if he did not make his way through he would "send the spark" out of him; and also, that he would put on a fire to force him. The boy at last stuck about the centre of an iron tube that ran along a lobby, at right angles with the chimney, which the witness stated was only 8½ inches wide, and at the extremity, where the boy was to be compelled to go through, it was only 4½ inches in diameter! When the witness found the boy he had been three hours in the tube, and he had to break the wall and get down the pipe before he could take him out. Having got down the pipe, the boy was so completely wedged into it that it took two men to pull him out. Bailie Lumsden, after hearing the above details, ordered the case to be taken before a higher court, as it was one of such atrocious cruelty as to merit a higher punishment than he was empowered to award.

GLASGOW HERALD 10 October 1834.

Climbing Boys. — Our attention has been frequently called to the pains suffered by a young and very unprotected class of the community, who follow an occupation at all times disagreeable and laborious, and one occasionally resulting in accidents of the most

The face of the under-privileged — a boy sweep.

fatal and cruel kind. We allude to the juvenile sweeps or climbing-boys, who perambulate our streets at morning's dawn, and since the occurrence of a recent and very painful case, in which a little fellow suffocated, after having cleaned more than thirty vents, public attention has more than once been directed to the subject. In some other cities this profession has been almost entirely put-down by the force of public opinion alone, and when the process of sweeping chimneys can be so easily managed by the rope and ball, or by other machinery, we hope the day is not distant when the plan of employing little creatures, who should rather be in an infant school than on the streets, will be altogether disused. The shrill cry of the sweep-boys, barefooted and scantily clad, almost at daybreak on the cold and biting mornings, break on the ear of the slumbering citizens, with a sound peculiarly painful, and if these children must work, surely there is some other line of industry into which they may pass, less pregnant with physical suffering. We have no intention of interfering with the bread-making of any class, but we can see no reason why the master sweeps should not use machinery rather than employ their own species in such a painful process. Even when unattended with the risk of severe accident, the profession is one of suffering and injury to health, as it is known that the constant covering of the skin with soot is productive of various painful cutaneous diseases. After the hint, therefore, we think the cause of humanity would be benefited by the formation of an association, having for its object the substitution of machinery for infant labour.

GLASGOW HERALD *24 February 1840.*

Accident to a Climbing Boy. — On Thursday evening about 7 o'clock, a little chimney-sweep, who was ordered by his master to ascend and cleanse a vent in Monteith Row, unfortunately stuck fast, in which disagreeable and dangerous predicament he remained upwards of an hour. The boy was at last released, without having sustained any serious injury.

GLASGOW HERALD *10 August 1840.*

Chimney-Sweeping. — It may not be out of place to prepare the public for the change, which, in the course of another year, will take place in the system of chimney sweeping. By the bill of last year, it is enacted that, from and after the first day of July 1842, any person who shall compel or allow a young person under 21 years of age to ascend or descend a chimney, or enter a flue, for the purpose of cleaning or coring it, or of extinguishing fire in it, shall be liable to a penalty of not more than £10 or less than £5. And it is also provided, that no person shall be apprenticed to the trade of chimney sweeping under the age of 16 years. It becomes necessary, therefore, that in the interval, men should be instructed in the use of the machine which is intended to supersede the operations of the climbing boys, and that the few chimneys which are unfit for the use of the machine should be altered, that the public may at once be guarded against inconvenience and danger.

GLASGOW HERALD *26 March 1841.*

———————————— * ————————————

DIVIDING THE SHEEP FROM THE GOATS

In compliance with an injunction of the Police Board, 31 little boys, selling shoe-ties, &c. on the streets, were pulled up by the police on Saturday night and lodged in the office. The allegation at the Police Board was, that these little fellows, while they were great annoyances on the street, were also pickpockets and thieves. On being inspected in the office, however, only two out of the 31 were known to the police as thieves — while from the statement of their parents, chiefly widows, the greater part of them appeared to be the means of supplying to the families with which they are connected, provisions for the Sunday. The banishment of these poor, and, as it appears, honest children, seems rather hard, though their solicitations on a Saturday evening are certainly annoying.

GLASGOW ARGUS 25 November 1839.

---------------- * ----------------

A CHILDHOOD IN DARKNESS

From Dixon's Govan Colliery comes the following picture of the work of the owner's toilers:

No. 6. Francis Connery, aged 9.

Is a trapper (i.e. opens and shuts the trapdoor ventilator when the hutches go past). He comes at 6 a.m. and goes at 6. He gets down and up by the engine. He sits on a board in a niche in the wall without a light, quite in the dark, and holds a rope which is fastened to the door, and when the carriage has passed he shuts it again. He has some bread, tea and cheese sent down by the engine and brought to him by a drawer, or if slack he can run and get it himself. It serves him for the day, as long as he is down the pit. He has not eaten all he got this morning yet. He sometimes falls asleep at his door when he is in the night shift: this is one week out of three. When he is asleep, the drawer raps at the door and he wakes and opens it. He gets 8d a day, and is "no able" to be a putter yet, but when he can he shall get 1s a day. His brother is a trapper here also, and is older than he is. Neither of them ever went to any school, day or night.

For the etiolated appearance of such a child the doctor to the Govan Colliery had a novel explanation. Some of the poor Irish children who lived near him, he said, and worked in the colliery were pale and ill-looking, but that was the fault, not of the labour, but of their parents, who did not feed them properly.

THE IRISH IN SCOTLAND. Handley, quoting the Children's Employment Commission Report of 1842.

---------------- * ----------------

THE LUXURIES OF YOUTH

When we who have grown, or are growing, grey were youngsters, a Penny was a lot of money, and there was nothing despicable in a

INDESTRUCTIBLE INDIA-RUBBER TOYS.

These toys consist of representations in miniature of elephants, horses, oxen, dogs, and indeed all the animals known by sight or hearsay to the denizens of the nursery, and are as remarkable for their artistic excellence as for their durableness. The figures are such exact copies from nature that only artistes could have made the moulds from which they were cast. As to their utility, of course, that quality consists in the fact that the toys cannot break, and that young Hopeful can crush them or let them fall from a height without damaging their symmetry. The dolls will gratify young Miss all the more that they are prettily dressed. Thousands to choose from.

THORNTON, CURRIE, & CO.,
INDIA-RUBBER MANUFACTURERS, WATERPROOFERS,
43, 45, AND 47 JAMAICA STREET, GLASGOW.

An advertisement for toys in 1879.

Ha'penny. A Sixpence was a fortune. I knew a boy who received that sum of money every week, and though I heard an old lady say he would come to a bad end, I envied him. Perhaps the bad end is waiting for him, but until now it would seem that his chief care in life has lain in taking care of the legacies that have at intervals befallen him, and I have seen nothing in his career to justify the old lady's prophecy. In 1880 old ladies did not wear hats, but that is no guarantee that they did not occasionally talk through their bonnets or lace caps.

To most of us, however, a Penny was the familiar coin, the same (as they say in modern business letters) being payable every Saturday. The Penny, though really a gratuity depending, theoretically, on the payee's good behaviour during the previous seven days, was never to my knowledge withheld; and, like older persons who have received gratuities for a considerable period, we had come to regard it as our right, and claimed it immediately after breakfast.

On Saturdays the people who kept sweetie shops in Hillhead became really alive. Mr. Ritchie, no doubt, was up betimes, preparing a stock of conical pokes to contain the purchases of his youthful customers — bull's eyes ("cheugh jeans"), toffee drops, slim-jim (a coconut confection in long strips), licorice "boot-laces", and many other delights, not forgetting his famed jujube-cuttings; Mr. Assafrey, too, had laid out ample supplies of his juvenile specialities — amazing pennyworths of broken chocolate and broken mixtures — one sometimes got a regular "plum" among the mixtures; while Messrs. Cooper & Co. had stacked up packages containing quarter-pounds of rose, musk and other lozenges, at 1d or 1½d each. . . .

Usually we bought sweeties that lasted, i.e. took time to consume. If we fell to temptations like the little chocolate creams, sixteen for a penny, rapture was brief and regret was long. Once, in that sudden madness which may attack even mature people with money to burn, my brother and I went it blind, pooling our pennies and speculating in Voice Jujubes, partly because they looked so nice, but mainly because the lady assured us that they were held in high esteem by vocalists, or, as she expressed it, "Singers is daft for them." Alas, it was not our lucky Saturday. The voice jujubes were exceeding tough and the taste, we thought, was horrid. We gave one to our parrot and awaited its bursting into song. Not a warble — only some abuse. So we presented the rest to Granny, an act which so touched her that she took from her petticoat her purse, and from her purse a sixpence, and — put in our bank. What a week-end!

I REMEMBER J. J. Bell. page 185.

HEALTH AND WELFARE

Nothing has changed so much, perhaps, over the last four centuries, as our knowledge of medicine and the care of the sick, and mentally ill. It is horrifying to read of the barbarous treatment meted out to the ill and helpless as recently as the early 19th century by otherwise intelligent and kindly people. Fear of contagion, of course, was an overriding reason for the drastic and often cruel measures taken against lepers and other sufferers in order to prevent the spread of disease in the city. As an inevitable result we find the quack doctors and their unfailing cures for every ailment under the sun — all miraculously available at 4s 6d a bottle! Senex gives a humorous account of them in his youth, and the gullibility of his contemporaries is confirmed by the advertisements of these rascals which continue to appear into the second half of the 19th century.

Victorian Glasgow combated disease by means of its remarkably advanced and pure water supply, introduced from the hills on the south in 1848, and from Loch Katrine, in 1859. The earlier water supplies are not so well known, so one has been introduced as a matter of interest. For the same reason, I have included a lethal recipe for the cure of the bite of a mad dog (not often required nowadays, luckily). This chapter ends with the crowning achievement of this city to medical science — the epoch-making discovery of an effective antiseptic by Joseph Lister in the 1860s. I cannot help feeling that this great achievement which has saved so many lives, is not remembered with the gratitude it deserves.

———————— * ————————

KEEPING OUT THE PEST

The proveist, baillies and counsall, conveinit for ordour taking with the pest, sieing it is incressit greitumlie in Edinburgh and vtheris pairtis in the cuntrey, hes thairfoir concludit and ordainit that the Stabillgrein port, Kirkport, Gallowgait, Tronegait and Kirk port and Schoolhous Wynd port, to be keipit be daylie watche be the inhabitantis of the quarteris according to the ordour vsit of auld, and to be nichtlie lokit; and siklyk hes concludit and ordainit that all the remanentis portis of this burgh be vpcloisit and all vther

passagis and yeardis endis; and that the portis be keipit be the maisteris of the hows in thair awin propir persounis allanarlie, to be keipit fra fyve houris in the mornyng to nyne houris at nycht.
EXTRACTS FROM THE BURGH RECORDS *10 August 1605.*

———————— * ————————

Item, it is statut and ordanit during this tyme of this greit infectioune of the pest in sindrie partis of the cuntrey that na travellouris or cadgeris cumand out of suspect places be resauit within this towne, and all vther personis cumand fra ony vthir places be nocht resauit without testimoniell. . . .
EXTRACTS FROM THE BURGH RECORDS *20 August 1606.*

———————— * ————————

The balleis and counsale convenit, vnderstanding that gret inconvenient may happin in this towne be travelouris, cadgeris, bakeris, and vtheris frequentand to Edinburgh, Sterling, Leithe, Air and vthir suspect placiss, and be travelouris cumand forth of the saidis pairtis to this towns, thairfoir it is statut and ordanit that na manir of persoune within this towne pas to the foirsaidis placiss or yit resaue ony manir of persoune cumand furthe thairof, vndir the paine of ten lib. and banischement of this towne.
EXTRACTS FROM THE BURGH RECORDS *21 August 1606.*

———————— * ————————

Tryell being tane of the seiknes in Archibald Muiris hows and Marioune Walker, his mother, and fund to be the plaige, ordanis to be askit of the said Marioune quha last frequentit with hir and quhat scheraris schewr with hir. And quhaevir beis inclosit or commandit in thair howssis be the balleis, quarter maisteris, or officeris, in thair names, that dissobeyis, to be haldin as pestiforus personis and transportit to the Muir with thair haill howshaldis and guidis. And ordanis all personis of this towne quha hes doggis or cattis that thai keipe thame fast or hang theme, vnder the paine of ten lib., and thame selfis to be inclosit. And ordanis all strainger begeris to depart of this towne incontinent, vndir the paine of scruging and burneing of them on the cheik and banischement, and quhaevir resaves them heireftir, or gifis thame harbrie within thair howssis, to be inclosit with thame and sustenit vpone thair expenssis as thai ar. . . .
EXTRACTS FROM THE BURGH RECORDS *20 September 1606.*

———————— * ————————

LEPERS

Injunctiounis and directiounis for the wattir serjand: — In the *first*, that he permit nane to be in the Lipper Hospitall bot sick as ar plaicit be the proveist and baillies and counsall, and that he mak thame thankfull and compleit payment of thair dewties and put thair wictuall to the heichest pryce, and that nane of thame be permitit to cum in the towne bot vpone Weddinsdaye and Settirday oulklie and that thai remaine na langer bot betuix ten houris and tua eftir noone, and that thai gang vpone the calsay syd with thair mussellis on thair faice, and clopperis, and that naine of thaime be permitit to beg at the kirk dor na dayis, and thair hows be keipit wattirfast.

EXTRACTS FROM THE BURGH RECORDS *15 October 1605.*

Jonet Gibson, seik lipper, vpone supplicatoun gifin in be hir befoir thee bailleis and counsale, is ordanit to be placit in the hospitall beyond the brig, be William Smyth, wattir setiand, scho behaveing hirself conforme to the statutis set down anent the seik lipper folk.

EXTRACTS FROM THE BURGH RECORDS *26 October 1611.*

---

*

A WELFARE CASE

The foirsaids magistratis and counsell, taking to thair consideratioun that Johne Duncane, elder, hemmerman, hes leived heirtofoir honestlie, being raither helpfull then burdeinsome, and now old decripped age being come vpon him, being past fourscoir yeires, and not able to work, as als being visite with povertie, at the pleasour of God, appoints him to be placed in Hutchesones Hospitall quhair he now lyes, the hous he had being brunt, and he to be interteinyeit thairine and the maister thairof to bestow vpon him suche allowance as is bestowit vpon vthers in the lyk conditioun and qualitie.

EXTRACTS FROM THE BURGH RECORDS *6 August 1653.*

---

*

Ordaines the master of work to pay to Adam Todd four dollars to help to pay the cure of James Todd, his son, who wes deadlie woundit at Killiecrankie.

EXTRACTS FROM THE BURGH RECORDS *13 January 1694.*

A CURE FOR THE BITE OF A MAD DOG

Take two Quarts of strong Ale, or if you cannot have Ale, wine; red Sage and Rue of each an handful and half, twelve Cloves of Garlick bruis'd; of Tin and Pewter scrap'd two Spoonfuls, of London Treacle (or Venice Treacle) an ounce; boil these close cover'd, till half consumed; stir in the Treacle when the rest is boiled; pour it into Bottles, cork it close, and it will keep a Year. Give three Spoonfuls Morning and Evening; one Pint English is succient for Man or Beast. Garlick, Rue and Salt pounded together may be applied to the Wound.

N.B. This Medicine has stood a Tryal of fifty Years Experience, and was never known to fail.

GLASGOW JOURNAL *10 August 1741.*

VITALINE.

The most wonderful discovery of the age, and the marvellous Vegeto-Tonic treatment for the cure and prevention of Biliousness, Sick Headache, Indigestion. Loss of Appetite, Tic Doloreux, Neuralgia, Nervousness, Giddiness, Scrofulous Affections, Ague, Debility, Spasms, and all derangements of the Stomach. By its administration the natural appetite is revived, and the functions of digestion and assimilation are improved, re-animated, and regulated ; and when its use has been steadily persevered in, its peculiar Tonic and Nutritive Powers have entirely restored Health and Strength to the most feeble and Shattered Constitutions.

VITALINE

Strengthens the whole muscular System, rouses into action the Physical Energy of the human frame, restores the long-lost Complexion, gives brilliancy to the Eye, a delightful fragrance to the Breath, and brings back sound and refreshing Sleep.

QUACKERY IN THE 18th CENTURY

. . . Of all the tricking practitioners in physic that ever set foot in Glasgow, by far the most impudent in quackery, and the most licentious in advertisements, was the celebrated Doctor James Graham, who made his appearance in this city in the year 1783. The Doctor (superior to most quacks) had two strings to his bow, for he solemnly averred that by his never-failing medicines, and by his scientific treatment of his patients, he not only prevented them from dying, but also by a wonderful discovery he had absolutely brought a new generation of beings into life, who would never have made their appearance in this busy world unless through his marvellous skill and all-potent agency. The Doctor, in his advertisements, styled himself "Doctor James Graham, President of the Council of Health, sole Proprietor and principal Director of the Temple of Health in Pall Mall, London". With reference to the first article of the doctor's grand curative treatment, it consisted of his celebrated *earth bath*, which, like Morrison's pills, cured all diseases. The patient, who was about to undergo the balneatory process, was first stripped naked, and then placed upon a glass stool, where he was electrified, by means of an electrifying machine. After being thus electrified, and well rubbed down with silken towels, he was plunged, or rather buried up to the mouth in an earth pit, the earth of it having been previously medicated by the doctor. Here the patient remained immured for the space of half an hour, when he was taken up, and being then cleaned and again well rubbed down, the sanitary process was completed.

But, however wonderful were the effects to the patients of a course of training through the medicines of the earth bath, these were thrown quite into the shade by the almost miraculous consequences which followed a sojourn in the Doctor's Temple of Health and Electric Bed. The Temple of Health was fitted up in a most gorgeous style, with silk rideaux, ottomans, mirrors, and chandeliers, and with every requisite of a bed-chamber which could render it snug and comfortable to the occupiers. The celebrated bed itself was adorned with elegant crimson silk damask curtains, having its coverlet and bedding also of silk. It was mounted upon four crystal pillars, and isolated so as that no part of the bed or bedding could touch the walls of the room, or could reach the carpet on the floor. In an adjacent apartment the Doctor had a powerful electrifying machine, from which machine to the bed there was maintained, during the whole course of the night, a constant stream of electricity, thereby keeping the bed always fully charged with this subtile fluid.

It is inconceivable how much curiosity was excited at this period in Glasgow to find out the names of any lodgers who had availed themselves of the benefits to be derived from the application of Dr. Graham's electric system; but notwithstanding of the most prying vigilance on the part of hundreds of our population, the Doctor managed his affairs so dexterously, that the public could never, with any degree of certainty, fix upon the names of any personages who had taken up their lodgings in the Temple of Health and Electric Bed. Amongst the most curious of the curiosity-peepers on this occasion was Bob Dreghorn, who might then have been seen at all times perambulating the streets in the immediate neighbourhood of the Doctor's abode, looking every suspicious person in the face, and then turning abruptly round for another short walk near the same spot — never, however, losing sight of it. But notwithstanding of all his prying watchfulness and circumspection, Bob was as much at fault as his neighbours, and never could tell who were the Doctor's customers. Some people alleged that Bob himself and a friend tried a night's lodgings with the Doctor; but this our eccentric townsman firmly denied.

GLASGOW PAST AND PRESENT *vol. II page 88.*

---

*

AN ECCENTRIC DOCTOR

The last personage who continued to walk these *Plain Stanes*, decked out with his scarlet cloak and cocked hat, was Dr. Peter Wright, whom your elderly readers no doubt will remember. The doctor's scarlet cloak, however, like the gowns of our senior collegians, was then getting rather threadbare, and had lost a little of its brilliant hue, so that I cannot say much for the learned gentleman's dignified appearance. There was another doctor in Glasgow in my younger days who was of rather an eccentric character. He might have been seen walking our streets, in a brown greatcoat, and supporting his left side with a crutch. This was Dr. Morris. This gentleman, it seems, took it into his head to try an experiment whether he or his horse could hold out longest upon a minimum of food; and, accordingly, he himself took just one raisin each day, and he allowed his horse only one straw daily. The consequence was, that his horse died, and the doctor lost the power of his left side; and what was, perhaps, even worse than that, he lost his patients, who very naturally said, "If the doctor tries such experiments upon himself, what will he not try upon us?"

GLASGOW PAST AND PRESENT *vol. I page 350.*

AN UNEXPECTED PRESENT

On the north our property was bounded by the property of Dr. Baird. His house was an old-fashioned house fronting the *Candleriggs*. This locality had not yet been dignified by the additional appellation of *street*. The doctor's house was entered by a long outside single stair which jutted upon the street. At the top of this stair there was a double door and a small wooden-framed cabin, which jutted upon the street, and was supported on the north by a stone pillar, the space below being open to the street. Behind this house was the doctor's garden, in which were some fine fruit trees. Now it so happened that one of those trees always bore large crops of apples, and some of its branches hung over our court in a most tempting manner. It is wonderful how all boys have a quick instinct, and an immediate intuitive perception of the Scotch law aphorism, "cujus est solum, ejus est usque ad coelum"; for whenever any fruit happens to project from a neighbour's grounds upon papa's grounds, every boy considers the fruit to belong to papa, as hanging in the heavens above his property; and so I argued in this case, and therefore felt no repugnance at throwing stones at the branches of this tree which overhung our court; but my motions were frequently carefully watched by Miss Betty Baird, the doctor's sister, from her bedroom window, which looked right upon the said tree. Now Miss Betty was a cankry old maid, and never failed to give me a most tremendous scolding whenever she found me transgressing; but I set her scolding at nought, as the apples which I brought down always fell on papa's ground, and there was a high stone wall between Betty and me.

There once happened rather a curious story connected with this apple tree. One of my brothers chanced early one morning to be going into our courtyard, when immediately below this said apple tree he found a man's leg, which he brought into our dining-room and laid it upon the table there, to the no small horror of the female part of our house. A grand consultation then took place amongst us, and the result was, that we concluded that Dr. Baird had been dissecting some dead subject, and that a dog had run off with the said leg and deposited it under the apple tree. Under this belief, the leg was sent to the doctor, with a notification of the circumstances under which it was found; but the doctor immediately returned the leg to us, saying that it was not *his* leg, and that he knew nothing about it. A second consultation now took place amongst us regarding how we should dispose of the leg. Some were for burying it in our own garden, while others were for sending it to the Council Chambers — there being no police office in those days in Glasgow for depositing *choses trouvées*. At last, however, we fixed upon sending it to the gravedigger of the Ramshorn burying-ground, with a message to him requesting him to bury it in the strangers' burying-ground. This plan was accordingly adopted, and the leg was despatched to the gravedigger with the necessary instructions. At this time there were several lairs in the Ramshorn burying-ground reserved for strangers, and on the walls which at one end enclosed them were printed in large characters: "Burying Ground for Strangers of Fashion". Now it so happened that we could not vouch that this leg belonged to a man of fashion; the gravedigger therefore declined giving it so honourable a place of sepulture, and unceremoniously buried it in some ignoble corner of the churchyard, where I presume it lies till this day.

GLASGOW PAST AND PRESENT *vol. II page 104.*

CRANSTONHILL WATER WORKS

THE COMPANY of PROPRIETORS of the CRANSTONHILL WATER WORKS beg leave to intimate to the INHABITANTS of the City of GLASGOW and SUBURBS, that as their FILTERING OPERATIONS and other WORKS are nearly finished, and their PIPES are laid in a number of the STREETS both of the CITY and SUBURBS, they will be able to supply FILTERED WATER in the course of a Month or Six Weeks.

As their Works have been carried on with the most rigid economy, they have fixed upon the following very moderate terms which are to continue to Whitsunday 1812.

The Inhabitants of any Street, so soon as the Company are ready to deliver Filtered Water in such Street, (of which due intimation shall be given,) shall be supplied for TWELVE MONTHS *gratis* from that date.

After the expiration of that space, Dwelling-Houses under £10 of rent shall be charged at 5s per ann.

Dwelling-Houses of £10 of rent and under £20 at 7s 6d. per ann.

And Dwelling-Houses of £20 of rent or upwards, at *Two* per cent per ann. upon the rent.

Public Works, Stables &c. will be supplied upon the most moderate terms, according to their consumpt of water.

GLASGOW HERALD *1 July 1808.*

Piped water — the latest convenience in 1825.

THE IRREPRESSIBLE WILLIAM HARLEY

In 1802, he procured a few acres of ground at Sauchyhall, merely for a family residence. It contained a great quantity of excellent Spring-water; and as the City then was very ill off for want of that necessary of life, . . . he got carts and four-wheeled carriages built, and sent a large supply of water into the City; which paved the way for the Glasgow and Cranstonhill Water Companies; these rendered the Willow Bank Water unnecessary, (from the rapid growth of golden and other Willows, he called the property he had acquired Willow Bank), and with a view to turn the water to account he erected the Baths; there were none in the City before.

. . . some invalids who came to bathe expressed a wish to have warm milk after bathing; to accommodate these a Cow was sent from Willow Bank to be milked at the Baths; this was the commencement of the Dairy. He improved, and cultivated to a considerable extent, waste land, and raised fruits and vegetables for the City; he also formed Arbours, and made walks of great extent and beauty; formed and planted the Square upon Blythswood Hill, &c.&c.

By the purchase and excambion of the Lands of Enoch Bank, he opened up St. Vincent Street, George Street, Renfrew Street, Bath Street, (by arches over a deep ravine, which was turned into ice-houses &c.) Nile Street and Renfield Street, and commenced building along several of those Streets, which was the commencement of what may be called the NEW TOWN. He also arched over and turned Enoch Burn into a common sewer . . . In 1810, the first Cow-house was built, which held twenty-four cows . . . as the demand for the milk increased, new buildings were erected, and at the peace there was accommodation for nearly 300 cows. . . .

GLASGOW HERALD *12 October 1827.*

KEEPING THE MENTALLY ILL OCCUPIED

To prevent the mind from brooding over morbid impressions, by affording to our Patients such means of employment as may serve to engage and to arrest attention, is an important part of our duty; and these means must be, in some measure, varied, according to the different habits of the Patients. Artisans, and others of the same rank, can generally be induced to betake themselves to such handicraft operations, as may without danger be permitted in the Asylum; or to the highly salutary exercise of labouring in the airing-grounds; while females of every rank have a ready resource against idleness, in their usual domestic employments. But males of the rank of gentlemen, who have learned no craft, and who would feel degraded, if employed in the humble operations of digging, or of wheeling, must, for the occupation of their tedious leisure hours, depend chiefly upon amusements; and, when convalescent, would feel their confinement to be peculiarly irksome, unless they were furnished with various appropriate modes of recreation. The game of billiards was, some years ago, introduced into the Asylum, and afforded much gratification to many of our Patients.

ELEVENTH ANNUAL REPORT OF
THE GLASGOW ASYLUM FOR LUNATICS 1825.

---

*

QUACK MEDICINES

To the Nervous and Consumptive, and those of debilitated Constitutions.

THE greatest and most valuable discovery of the present age is universally allowed to be the Celebrated *Cordial Balm of Buekia, or Prolonger of Life*, which is a certain and effectual Remedy for Nervous Disorders, Juvenile Indiscretions, Lowness of Spirits, Female Complaints, Headache, Debility, Loss of Appetite, Relaxations, Indigestion, Coughs and Cold, Bilious Cases, Consumption, Asthma, Gout in the Stomach, Impurities of the Blood,&c. Prepared only by the sole Proprietors.

DRS. H. BECK & CO. may be consulted, as usual, every day, at their House, 127, Argyll Street, opposite the Arcade, Glasgow, and Patients in the remotest parts of the country be treated successfully, on describing minutely the

The Quack Doctor with his cure for every ailment.

case, and enclosing a remittance for Advice and Medicine, which can be forwarded to any part of the world. No difficulty can occur, as the Medicines will be securely packed, and carefully protected from observation. . . .

The Cordial Balm of Buekia is pleasant to the taste and smell; its softening, healing, and tonic qualities, afford, by perseverance in its use, a certain prospect of returning strength to those who are debilitated by premature or excessive indulgencies.

Sold in Bottles at 4s 6d and 11s each, or two 11s Bottles in one, 20s each, or four quantities in one family Bottle, at 33s, duty included, whereby one 11s Bottle is saved.

Drs. H BECK & CO., for nearly fifteen years, have been devoted to an exclusive practice in those diseases which, in various forms, assail the victim of private folly or public intemperance, and with confidence invite the afflicted to make trial of their invaluable preparations, which will be found a most effectual cure for all diseases of a secret nature, whether arising from improper treatment or neglect.

GLASGOW FREE PRESS *26 February 1834.*

————————— * —————————

DRS. MOORE have, with great anxiety, observed that Scorbutic and other Eruptive Disorders have very considerably increased in this country of late years, notwithstanding the many remedies which have been repeatedly offered to the public under the most specious pretences. The merits of these specifics it is not their business or intention to call in question. They cannot, however, but regret, that after the strenuous efforts of so many persons attentive to the cure of these complaints, and the whole Materia Medica having been ransacked for the means to eradicate them, they should still gain ground, and become, in a manner, constitutional to numbers of the inhabitants of this climate. . . .

The Public have therefore been presented with Drs. Moore's PURIFYING ANTI-SCORBUTIC DROPS, a most safe, salutary, and absolute specific Remedy for those deplorable and hitherto incurable diseases, viz.:— *Scurvy, Leprosy, Elephantiasis, King's Evil, Scrofula, Struma, Erysipelas, or St. Anthony's Fire,* &c. In every stage of those Disorders, where Salivation has repeatedly failed, when no other remedy could restore the unhappy sufferer to that health he unfortunately lost, the PURIFYING ANTI-SCORBUTIC DROPS will be found the only effectual and radical remedy to re-establish health and vigour.

Sold in bottles, with the Proprietor's name blown on the outside of the bottles, at 3s.6d., or four in one for 11s. or two 11s. for 20s.; with directions, and a treatise relative to the complaint, at 25, George's Square, West, Glasgow. Where also may be had Drs. Moore's TOOTH TINCTURE, an infallible cure for the Toothache in one minute without drawing. Price 2s.9d. and 7s. per bottle. — Drs. Moore's ITCH OINTMENT, a cure guaranteed for the Itch, in one application, price 1s.9d. per box.

Dr. Moore and Co. invite all classes of the community, who may suffer from Sore Legs, Scalded Heads, Old Wounds, or Sores on any part of the body, Scorbutic Eruptions, &c., however obstinate, or of long standing, and he pledges the high reputation he has acquired in every part of Europe, that he will cure, to the satisfaction of all applicants, any of the above, in a time incredibly short, by using his, Dr. Moore's, Golden Ointment.

Sold in Boxes at 2s.9d. and 4s.6d., accompanied by full and explicit directions, by which persons may cure themselves, at Dr. Moore and Co.'s Establishment. . . .

GLASGOW FREE PRESS *22 March 1834.*

--------------------- * ---------------------

CHOLERA EPIDEMICS

Cholera had visited Glasgow in 1832, but in the scourge of 1849 the mortality was appalling, equalling in ratio that of the later Crimean war. Wallace, from whose *Popular History of Glasgow* I draw records "the indignant outcry from the people regarding the reckless manner in which the bodies of the dead were buried, and the overcrowded condition of the burial grounds." . . .

It was under such distressing sanitary conditions that Lister first put into practice his antiseptic treatment; and while more hopeless conditions could scarcely well be imagined, or afford a man stern and crucial test, Lister, assured in his own mind of the remedial qualities and effects of his ultimately acclaimed and now universally accepted treatment, steadfastly persevered in the face of much medical and other opposition. He was doing for humanity, what Florence Nightingale had done at Scutari for the Crimean wounded. . . .

REMINISCENCES OF LISTER *Sir Hector Cameron.*

COLD STATISTICS

In December 1853, and the whole of 1854, Glasgow suffered terribly from the ravages of Asiatic cholera. During those thirteen months no fewer than 3,885 deaths took place, and the utmost consternation prevailed in the community.

HISTORY OF GLASGOW *MacGregor. 1881. page 443.*

---------------- * ----------------

PERSONAL SUFFERING

. . . An *actual* scene now draws attention. We are still in this afflicted neighbourhood, the Bridgegate. Two policemen, accompanied by a crowd of people, are making their way towards us, the former carrying a stretcher. It is covered over with a sheet of canvas, and idle curiosity is stimulated to know the cause of the sorrowful procession. It stops at the mouth of a close, when suddenly more than two score of ragged spectators, chiefly women, are collected together. . . . With some difficulty the policemen reach the bottom of the stair where the family reside. The lad, about fourteen years of age, is uncovered, and his sickly, death-like aspect sends a pang to every heart. His clothes are dirty, thin, and ragged. For a moment the policemen wait the mother's expected arrival. She has gone in quest of her boy to the police station. Proceeding with him up a narrow wretched stair, a few kind neighbours show the poor woman's home. It is one room, comparatively large and clean, with no furniture except a chest, a stool, and a little broken crockery. In a corner, however, is a filthy tick, half-filled with straw. Upon this the lad is laid, trembling with cold, writhing in pain with cramp, and prostrate by a weakening attack of diarrhoea. Some dirty rags, and remnants of clothes from anywhere, are collected, and thrown over him. The stench and closeness of the room are indescribable. It is full of low gossipping women, easing their hearts by expressions of sorrow. Suddenly an Irish woman, somewhat advanced in years, makes her appearance along the narrow passage. She is frantic with grief, and as she enters, wringing her hands, asks for her "poor boy". In a moment she is on her knees, embracing him with a wild affection. What is the history of the case, and what is to be done? The policeman tells us that the lad had fallen down in the street, and was removed to the office, where he had been for two hours. What medical attention he received there, no one can tell. Here he is brought in agony to a poor helpless distracted mother. No one knows where to get a medical attendant, or how to procure the means to purchase brandy or medicine. Out of about fifty persons we do not believe a single sixpence could have been raised. Suggesting the clearing of the room, fresh air is at once admitted; and in a few minutes more we have the satisfaction to see . . . one or two little wants supplied, which the urgency of the case renders necessary. From several visits subsequently paid, we found that the whole neighbourhood had become more or less affected with attacks of a similar kind — viz., British Cholera. The boy, however, recovered, and we trust is now the comfort of his poor widowed parent.

MIDNIGHT SCENES AND SOCIAL PHOTOGRAPHS. *1858*
(1976 Reprint page 44).

In need of care and attention.

EATING
AND SHOPPING

Calvinistic attitudes did not encourage the culinary art, and frugality was the chief virtue of a 17th-century housewife. Eating out was not advisable except when travelling. In this respect Margaret Hamilton's "cookerie" seems to be the earliest recorded Glasgow restaurant. By 1740 ideas had progressed sufficiently for the Town Council to encourage James Lochhead's school of cookery for young ladies who wanted to improve the standard of their entertainments. At the same time shops began to appear, replacing the old markets where at one time all the shopping was done. The curious advertisements couched in the quaint (to us!) language of the period, give a picture of an age long disappeared. In the following century development was swift with the appearance of such novelties as shopping arcades and department stores. In the home, gas began to be used for cooking, although it was many years before the old ranges fell into disuse. The culmination of the century's progress was reached with the appearance on the streets of tea and coffee dispensers cunningly disguised as lamps!!

---------------- * ----------------

THE FIRST RESTAURANT?

In answer to the supplication given in be Margaret Hamilton, cook, craving libertie to continow in the said employment for serveing the inhabitants with meat and drink, at the ordinary tymes of dyets, as likewayes strangeris, and not to be discharged to doe the same, for the reasones contained in the said petition, the magistrats and toune counsell doe allow and ordaine the said Margaret Hamilton to continow and exerce her said employment as formerlie, and nominats and appoints the dean of gild and deacon conveener to meet with her and try what she will give to the toune for getting the said libertie allowed her for keeping of ane taverne and ane cookerie in tyme comeing, dureing her lifetyme, and to report.

EXTRACTS FROM THE BURGH RECORDS 15 May 1691.

SCHOOL OF COOKERY

Anent the petition given in by James Lochhead, teacher of cookery, mentioning that he being regularly educated by his Majesty's cooks, under whom he served in the art of cookery, pastry, confectioning, candying, preserving and pickling, and of making of milks, creams, syllabubs, jellies, soups and broaths of all sorts, and also taught to dress and order a table and to make bills of fare for entertainments of all kinds, and that of late he has successfully taught severall young ladies to their oun and their parents satisfaction, and that for instruction of his scholars he is obliged to provide, upon his own charge, flesh, fowles, fish, spiceries and severall other ingredients, but when dresst lye on his hand for want of sale, by which he is a loser and will be obliged to lay aside his teaching unless he be assisted in carying it on, and therefore craving a yearly allowance for his encouragement; which being considered by the magistrats and councill they remitt to the magistrats to agree with him upon the terms and conditions of his teaching, and he to be allowed £10 sterling yearly for his encouragement during pleasure, commencing from and after Whitsunday next, and the magistrats to draw precepts upon the thesaurer therefore.

EXTRACTS FROM THE BURGH RECORDS 8 *May 1740*.

---- * ----

This is to give Notice

That JAMES LOCHHEAD *who was educated by his Majesty's Cooks at London, and did afterwards officiate with them for several Years, has for some Time past kept a School at his House above the Cross, opposite to Bell's Wynd, where he teaches* COOKERY *and* PASTRY, *in all their Parts; as also Pickling, Preserving, Candying, making of Jellies, Syllabubs, and the different Ways of dressing Milks, Creams, Roots, Herbs, and Fruits of all Kinds: As, also, how to dress up anew any Sort of Cold Meat left at Dinner or Supper, in such a Manner, that none but a Person of the nicest Taste can distinguish it from Meat newly drest as it came from the Mercat.*

He teaches likewise Jointing and Carving of Meat, Fowls &c. of all Kinds, with the newest Manner of Laying a Cloath, and folding Napery: and several other Things too tedious to mention, tho' very useful for most families.

He proposes in a Month's Time to make any Young Lady who gives Application, fit to oversee and give Directions to Servants about any of the above Articles, for which he takes only 10 Shillings.

He is willing to attend any who please to employ him at their own Houses, for dressing and ordering Entertainments of any kind, which he has often done to the Satisfaction of Persons of the first Quality. He begins to teach for this Season on the 10th Instant, and will give closs Attendance. Any who cannot attend his School may be taught with great Care at their own Lodgings.

He furnishes one or more Dishes drest in the most genteel and frugal Manner, at any Time of the Day, to such as call for them out of the House: and any who please to come to his House, shall be entertain'd at the most reasonable Rates.

GLASGOW JOURNAL 5 October 1741.

———————— * ————————

ROBERT McNAIR'S GROCERY SHOP

JUST IMPORTED

And to be sold by Robert McNair and Company at their Shop opposite to the Main Guard, and at their Warehouse in the Candlerigs.

A Parcel of Limons, Olive Oil, Raisens, Figs, Prunes and Currants, with a fine Assortment of the newest Fashion'd and best Patterns of Dishes and Plates, Stone and Delph Tea Cups and Saucers of sundry Kinds: with a Parcel of the newest Fashion'd double and single Wine, Dram and Beer Glasses; and different Sorts of Glass and Stone Decanters; with sundry Kinds of Spiceries and Spirits. Also a fine Parcel of Chopin Bottles, with three Sorts of Pint Bottles; and several other Kinds of Grocerie ware, all to be sold as cheap as by any either in this Town, Edinburgh or Leith; and Encouragement will be given to any who buy in the Wholesale Way.

N.B. Any Person may be served at Burials with Glasses, Tankards and Salvers for Sixpence each Burial; and poor People may be served Gratis. The Shop will be every Day kept open from Eight in the Morning to Nine at Night.

GLASGOW JOURNAL 28 September 1741.

THERE is come Home, and to be sold by Robert McNair, opposite to the Main Guard, Glasgow, A Parcel of Lintseed which came Home in the Ship Agnes of Renfrew, in the Month of July last, from Campvere, Any Gentlemen who wants to purchase may send for Samples of it, and try it. And I further oblige myself, that, if it do not grow, to return the Money they gave for it, and to give an Obligation in Writing for the same at delivery. 'Tis to be sold at twenty one Shilling Scots the Peck, and at twenty five Pound Scots the Hoghead, and at twenty Six Pounds Scots at four Months Trust.

ROBERT McNAIR.

N.B. I received an Account of a Parcel of Potatoes being shipt for me from the West of England, which will answer for Seed, or eating. I expect them, if the Wind holds South West, in four days and a Half.

GLASGOW JOURNAL 19 April 1742.

———————— * ————————

MARKET DUES

John Wilson and John Orr, town clerks, in obedience to the act of council of 20th June last, reported that they had made dilligent enquiry concerning dues payable to the city of Glasgow, and in use to be levied by their tacksmen of their fish and potatoe mercates, flesh mercate, for butter, milk and eggs brought into the city, for the use of the citys washing house in the Green of Glasgow, and for the cran and quay at Broomielaw of Glasgow, and that they had examined several of the old tacksmen of the above mentioned mercates . . . with respect to the dues upliftable by them of old and of late as tacksmen of these different subjects, and that they had made out tables of the fees thereof agreeable to the information they had received. . . .

Each single cart loaded with fish pays 1s. sterling, each horse load of fish pays 6d. sterling, each burden of fish on a persons back or on a barrow pays 3d. sterling; and all fish sold in private houses pay as if sold in the mercate; each large or double cart load of potatoes pays 1s. sterling, each single cart load of potatoes pays 6d. sterling, each horse load of potatoes pays 3d. sterling, each burden or barrow full of potatoes pays 1½d. sterling; and all potatoes sold privately within the royalty of the city pay the same dues as if sold in the public mercate.

Each cow pays 6d. sterling, each sheep pays 1d. sterling, each lamb pays ½d. sterling, each sow pays 2d. sterling, each goat pays 1d. sterling, and each calf 1d. sterling.

Each barrel of butter milk pays ½d. sterling, and one egg is due from each basket or creel of eggs.

For a days washing of a woman in a tub 3d. sterling; if any person assist by what is called rubbing 1d. sterling more is paid; for a half days washing of woman in a tub 2d. sterling, and there is no additional charge for a rubber in the last case, for washing the smallest article 1d. sterling, each days washing of a woman pays for watching 1½d. sterling. N.B. No watching of the smallest article below 1d. For each copper boiling with cloath or cloaths 6d. sterling, for each 2 pails of warm water for synding or steeping ½d. sterling, for each pair of blankets washing or scouring ½d. sterling.

Each vessel or boat pays for each ton 1d. sterling, each hogshead of sugar pays of cranage dues tho' the cran be not used 2d. sterling, if the cran be used each hogshead of sugar pays 1d. sterling more; each ton of hemp pays of cranage tho' the cran be not used 4d. sterling, if the cran be used, hemp pays 2d. sterling more per ton, in all 6d. sterling; each large hogshead of tobacco, if the cran be used, pays 3d. sterling, each small hogshead of tobacco, if the cran be used, pays 2d. sterling; but no dues are payable for tobacco except when the cran is used.

EXTRACTS FROM THE BURGH RECORDS 12 September 1781.

———————————— * ————————————

JAMES KIRKWOOD

At the Lemon Tree and two Sugar Loaves, third shop west from the Bull, Glasgow,

HAS just got to hand a large quantity of very fine

APPLES AND PEARS, VIZ.

Golden Pippins
London Pearmains
Winter Johnies
Winter Pearmains
Scarlet, Russet, and
Green Apples.

Swan Egg Pears
Eating Pears
Stewing ditto.
Green Pearmains
Golden Rennet Apples
Large Russets

Teas of different kinds, at the lowest prices. Sugars, Wines, &c., and Whisky at 1s. 10d. per pint. Also, a fresh assortment of very fine Bacon Hams. Commissions from the country carefully answered.

GLASGOW MERCURY *17 February 1785.*

TEAS

Just arrived from the India-House, at the reduced prices.

ANDREW and ROBERT THOMSON, head of New Wynd, Trongate, beg leave to inform their customers, and the public, that they have just got to hand, from London, (purchased at the last tea-sale) a large and well assorted parcel of fresh high-flavoured Teas, consisting of Bohea, Congou, Sauchong, Hyson, and Common Greens, (warranted unmixed) which they are selling considerably under the former prices.

Also, Coffee and Chocolate, Marmalade and Jellies, French Plumbs, and Jar Raisins, Valentia and Faro Almonds, Spiceries, Sugars, and Confections, Wines and Spirits, with a general assortment of other Groceries, at the lowest prices, for ready money.

N.B. Continue to make, as formerly, Seed-Cake, Plumb-Cake, Diet-Loaves, and Biscuits of all Kinds, for retail, or furnished for funerals, on the shortest notice.

GLASGOW MERCURY *24 February 1785.*

TURTLE SOUP

MRS HEWIT, ALBION TAVERN, No. 131, Trongate, returns thanks for the liberal encouragement she has received since commencing business, and begs to intimate to her friends and the public, that she has procured a TURTLE, which will be cooked on Wednesday first, the 6th instant.

Soups, Steaks, &c., as usual, every day.

Ales and Porter from the Butt. — Newspapers.

GLASGOW HERALD *4 June 1827.*

THE ARGYLE ARCADE —
A NEW WAY TO SHOP

We are happy in having it in our power to announce the near completion of this beautiful and interesting place of business. Every attention appears to have been paid to the comfort and luxury of those possessing the premises, and also of those who visit them, in order to transact the daily business of life. . . .

The situation is admirably adapted for an establishment of the kind, being a communication between Argyll and Buchanan Streets, two of the leading or principal Streets in Glasgow, forming an obtuse angle at the centre, running in from Argyll Street half the extent of the passage, and then turning into Buchanan Street. The idea of the thoroughfare appears to be taken from the many passages of a similar description in Paris, other cities on the Continent, and the Burlington Arcade in London; but for simplicity of style, elegance, and lightness, we believe the Argyll Arcade exceeds any that have yet been completed. The Burlington is larger, but two or three feet narrower, and the roof is more enclosed, there being only about one-fifth of the whole glass; whereas the Glasgow Arcade is almost entirely one sheet of latticed glass-work, and the ventilation very complete; so much so, that from its construction it forms the coolest Shade in summer, and will be comfortably sheltered in winter.

The style of the entrance from Argyll Street is a handsome arched gateway, supported on two massive Doric columns, the interior being a continuation of the same simple style of architecture, so far as it could be applied; and the roof, supported by pilasters, forming the divisions or fronts, of the shops; the entire space betwixt these pilasters being filled with glass, forming the doors and windows of the shops, with neat airy parlours or places of business on the second range. The roof is about 35 feet high, and has a very striking effect when there is a ray of sunshine from the trellis or latticed divisions, with the regular beams and bracings, forming a beautiful chequered canopy of glass. The windows of the shops are large and spacious, and that uniformity has been preserved throughout which gives an entireness to the whole, without being heavy or dull.

The entrance from Buchanan Street is also through a handsome archway, which, with the balconies on each side, and the veranda in front, gives a light elegant appearance. When the whole is finished and painted, we have no doubt but it will become one of the most frequented places of business in Glasgow, from its cleanness, the comfort of shopping under cover, in all kinds of weather, and the regulations for the attention of the gate-keepers and watch, preventing many obstructions and inconveniences to be met with in

the open streets. We understand the shops are nearly all let; and there is such variety as almost to preclude the necessity of leaving the Arcade for any article that may be wanted.
GLASGOW HERALD *11 July 1828*.

---

*

Argyll Arcade ... Where, in particular, the comfort and convenience of Ladies who resort to it has been so much studied, and where amusement is combined with utility, we have little doubt but it will be found attractive. The place will form an agreeable promenade in every kind of weather. Those arriving in carriages may be set down at the one end, and the carriages be sent round to take up the company at the other.
GLASGOW HERALD *14 July 1828*.

---

*

FEEDING THE STARVING

Soup Kitchens. — We are happy to observe that we now have got soup-kitchens in different districts of the city, where good and substantial broth and bread are supplied to the needy. What though a few impositions should take place? Can this at all stand against the real benefit which is conferred on many a poor though industrious family? But, by the by, there can surely be no imposition whatever, for if a comfortable diet be a preventive from cholera (and we are willing to allow it is a most capital medicine), the worthless, for the sake of the community, should also be largely supplied with the sovereign specific. — It would be invidious to be particular where all are doing their duty, but we cannot help calling attention to the plan of the "Barley Broth Kitchen" in Great Clyde Street — (see advertisement) — where every thing appears to be conducted in the very best style, and where six hundred quarts of broth are distributed daily. We were well pleased with a rule adopted by Mr. Menzies, of the kitchen belonging to the eleventh ward. Seeing that many of those who came for the soup were extremely dirty in their persons, a quantity of soap was issued to each of the customers, with a gentle hint that no more broth would be given unless they could keep themselves always very cleanly washed. It is needless to say that the hint was taken, — and nothing can now be more gratifying than to see the young ones trigly (*neatly*) dressed and clean, proudly marching home to their grateful parents, with their allowance of bread and smoking canfuls of "Cholera Preventive".

BARLEY BROTH KITCHEN,
19, GREAT CLYDE STREET.

LADIES and GENTLEMEN wishing to purchase Tickets for distribution will please enter their names any day of the week previous to the one for which the supply is required. Subscription Books are to be found at Messrs. Lumsden and Son's, Queen Street; Mr. J. Graham's, 90, Argyll Street; Mr. Murray, baker, Upper Buchanan Street; and with Mr. Russell, at the kitchen.

Tickets for One Ration of Broth & Bread, 6d. p. week.

Tickets for Two Rations of Broth & Bread, 1s. p. week.

Tickets for Three Rations of Broth & Bread, 1s 6d. p. week.

Tickets for Four Rations of Broth & Bread, 2s. p. week.

No single Tickets can be disposed of; and on no account will a supply be given except on the days specified on the weekly Tickets.

To meet the wants of Tradesmen out of Employment, Strangers, or others who may not wish to apply for Tickets gratis, a limited number will be on Sale every Saturday at the Kitchen.

N.B. As the quantity of Broth, and quality of Bread, considerably exceed in value the Prices charged, Donations in money, or Produce, useful for the Kitchen, will be thankfully received.

GLASGOW HERALD *2 March 1832.*

—————————— * ——————————

Cucumbers and Gooseberries, the first this season, were yesterday exposed in Mr. Thomson's early fruit shop, Trongate. One shilling and sixpence for the Cucumbers, and one shilling and fourpence a pint for the Gooseberries, was the price asked.

GLASGOW COURIER *20 May 1834.*

THE FIRST GLASGOW LIFT?

OPENING OF
MESSRS. WYLIE & LOCHHEAD'S
NEW ESTABLISHMENT
45, BUCHANAN STREET.

This establishment, in which stone, timber, iron and glass have contributed, under the hands of the builder and decorator to form an erection alike unique and magnificent, was opened for the first time on Monday last, the 2d. current, for the sale of every article connected with house furnishing. For extent and beauty, it surpasses, as a place of business, anything of which we have seen or heard, — a sentiment which we believe is shared by vast numbers of our citizens who have visited the premises during the last three days, and who are unanimous in their expressions of admiration of the magnitude of the building, and of the exquisite style with which the whole has been got up. The building, which extends from Buchanan Street to Mitchell Street, is upwards of two hundred feet in length, sixty-three feet in breadth, and seventy feet in height from the floor to the cupola. It consists of a spacious street floor, and three lofty open galleries, rising one above another, and extending round the whole building in a semi-circular form. A magnificent cupola of ground glass, extending the whole length of the galleries, throws down a perfect flood of light, but at the same time so well subdued and tempered as to fall softly all around, and exhibit with the best effect the elaborate decorations of the structure, and the goods of every kind and hue with which it is so abundantly stored.

We have no space to enter into details regarding this commercial Crystal Palace; for the public may judge for themselves, but we may notice a very ingenious hoisting apparatus, worked by a neat steam engine, which is intended not only to lift up the bales from the waggon entrance to the uppermost parts of the building, but to elevate those ladies and gentlemen to the galleries to whom the climbing of successive flights of stairs might be attended with fatigue and annoyance. Parties who are old, fat, feeble, short-winded, or simply lazy, or who desire a bit of fun, have only to place themselves on an enclosed platform or flooring, when they are elevated by a gentle and pleasing process, to a height exceeding that of a country steeple; and from the railing of the upper gallery, they may look down on a scene of industrial activity and artistic magnificence which as yet has not a parallel amongst us. . . .

Beautiful as it is during the day, this establishment is no less attractive at night, from the complete and chaste style in which the lighting is arranged — there being nearly 200 gas lights with their globes appropriately and harmoniously dispersed throughout the place.

GLASGOW HERALD 6 *April* 1855.

A Lipton advertisement of 1879.

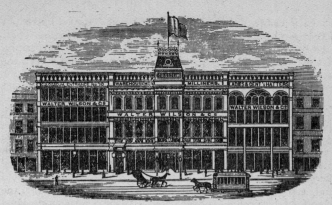

GENTLEMEN'S FELT & DRESS HAT DEPARTMENT.

2,500 BOYS' TWEED TAM O' SHANTERS, for 10½d each
To those with a family of Boys, they are what is wanted.

WALTER WILSON & CO.,
The Leading Hatters,

A Colosseum advertisement of 1880.

THE COLOSSEUM

This week Mr. Walter Wilson will open an important addition which has been made to the Colosseum warehouse. This consists of a spacious building, erected on the Broomielaw, to accommodate what may be described as a new departure in connection with the trade of the Colosseum. The event is rather an interesting one, for the reason that it marks a stage in the progress of a business which has attracted a good deal of attention from the rapidity with which, from a comparatively small beginning, it has grown to very large proportions. The Colosseum had its origin about 16 years ago when Mr. Wilson opened a shop in Jamaica Street with a staff of 20 hands. Gradually the business increased, and as a consequence the premises were extended. Bit by bit the surrounding warehouses were absorbed, until at the present time the Colosseum occupies no fewer than six large blocks of building varying from four to five storeys in height, and the employees number 400. There are 30 distinct departments, and, as indicating the extent of the accommodation, it may be stated that the fittings comprise literally miles of counter and shelving. Owing to the manner in which the premises were extended, they did not present that regular appearance internally which is so necessary for the success of such a business as that carried on by Mr. Wilson, and accordingly some time ago operations were begun with a view to the remodelling of the warehouse. These have been nearly completed, the result being highly satisfactory. Means of easy communication have been opened up between the various departments and the first floor has been reduced to one level, so that there is an uninterrupted stretch of 100 yards right through the five blocks facing Jamaica Street.

The building in the Broomielaw which will this week be thrown open to the public, forms rather an important addition to the architecture of the street. In general style the front elevation accords with that of the other premises occupied by Mr. Wilson. Although to some people it may be a matter of regret that the building operations have rendered necessary the destruction of an old landmark — the Lord Byron Hotel — it must be admitted that the amenity of the locality has been improved. The removal of the hotel too has given the authorities an opportunity of levelling the street at this particular point. The new warehouse, which is to be known as the Scottish Wholesale Stores, is a substantial structure consisting of four storeys and basement. The floor on the street level has been laid out as a handsome shop with three doors and large plate-glass windows. The other flats are also well-lighted, and are arranged in such a way as to give great space for the accommodation of customers. The levels have been made to correspond with those of the Jamaica Street buildings, and ample means of inter-communication have been provided so that practically the whole six blocks form one large warehouse. Regarding the branch of business that will be carried on at the Broomielaw, ... it will be of a somewhat different character from that which has made the Jamaica Street establishment so well known. A trade will be done in any article of merchandise that can be bought to advantage in large quantities, the principle adopted in the Civil Service Stores, London, being followed, namely, an immense turnover and small profits. . . .

GLASGOW HERALD 20 April 1885.

———————— * ————————

INGENIOUS 'CASH' ARRANGEMENT IN A GLASGOW WAREHOUSE

There was inaugurated on Wednesday in the warehouse of Messrs. Arnott & Co., Jamaica Street, one of the most ingenious contrivances of recent times. It is what is known as the "Lamson Cash Railway," which, although extensively used in the stores and warehouses of the United States and Canada, has never before been seen in practical operation in Scotland. The purpose of the "railway" is to convey safely, promptly, and accurately from any part of a large warehouse to the cashier's box the money received in payment of goods, and to return, with the same expedition, the change, if any, and vouchers. In short, it supersedes the hitherto indispensible "cash boy," who is described by the promoters of the new system as vexatious and unreliable, and substitutes a medium which, it is claimed, is free from all objectionable features, and has given great satisfaction in America.

As seen in practical working in Messrs. Arnott's warehouse, the Lamson system consists of a series of elevated miniature railways in lines radiating to the different flats and departments from the cashier's box, which is near the centre. There are 12 separate lines, and they pass over the various counters so as to serve every part of the warehouse. There are two tracks on each line — a high level and a low level track — and one is inclined towards the cashier's desk, while the other is inclined in the opposite direction. The money lifted at a given counter is put inside hollow balls, which are lettered and marked, and these being put on the former track find their way to the cashier's desk in a few moments. They are returned with the change and vouchers by the other track quite as expeditiously. The balls are of different sizes, and are graduated to work "switches" on the various lines, and by this means each ball finds its proper track. The "switches" are made use of on four diverging lines, which connect with the main lines, eight in number. Of the advantages of the new system to shoppers, as well as the salesmen, there cannot be any difference of opinion. It effects a considerable saving of time, abates the excitement always apt to occur in a large warehouse, and works noiselessly and with perfect accuracy. So far as Wednesday's experience went the "railway" was an entire success.

GLASGOW HERALD 3 July 1885.

———————— * ————————

EARLY GAS COOKERS

SIR, — My attention was lately directed to this new method of cooking by gas, so prettily described in a Paisley paper in the account of a dinner given to a Mr. Millar by the Gas Company there; but, as I considered it only as a nice experiment, I thought no more of it till a few days ago, when we had a gentleman from Edinburgh dining with us, who informed me that these gas ovens were now in daily use in Edinburgh, and were found to answer admirably — so much so, that a Mr. Milne was now making a business of it; and he showed me one of Mr. Milne's circulars, with an engraving and description of the machine. It was so simple and ingenious, and requiring only a pennyworth of gas to roast a joint of meat, and make ready potatoes at the same time, that I instantly resolved to have one. He likewise mentioned that the gas was used for heating rooms, and even churches, and that it was not much dearer than coal, if we took into account the extra cleaning, and the injury to fine furniture from the smoke and dust occasioned by coal fires. Being fond of all new improvements, before the gentleman left us I sent for a workman to give him instructions about what I wanted him to make. After hearing me, he answered, with an arch smile, "They may do very well in Edinburgh, but I doubt they'll no do here; for you will neither get heat nor light from our Company till it's dark, and that'll be owre late to begin to cook a dinner; for the Company here stop off the gas from their pipes till the time of lighting." At this announcement the gentleman smiled, and observed, "That is because you have no opposition; they treat the public as they please; but it is not so with us in Edinburgh. Since we got the opposition Company, the public has been treated with the utmost civility, and we have gas at all hours." . . .

Now, Sir, would it not be worth while to have another Company in Glasgow likewise, so as we might supply ourselves with gas for the purposes of heating and cooking? I think if such a work was begun about the cotton factories at Bishop-street, or the ground near the canal road, and the pipes carried up Blythswood-hill, the most of the families would take it in, it would be so clean and nice; nay, I was thinking of having it brought to the dining and tea table (by Milne's flexible pipes, as in Edinburgh), to keep the dishes warm. I assure you, Sir, it would really be a luxury to have each nice slice hot as from the fire; besides, the tea vase, coffee, eggs, rolls, muffins, &c., every thing could be had in season, and to perfection; the temperature of the rooms would be so equal with the comfort of a continual blazing fire, and no smoke or dust to injure the furniture or paintings, and many other advantages that I could enumerate, but I am afraid I tire your patience; only I would wish some of the gentlemen, who understand these things better, would set it agoing, and oblige the ladies of Blythswood-hill.

M. CHILD.

GLASGOW FREE PRESS 7 May 1834.

GAS STOVES

The PARTICK, HILLHEAD and MARYHILL GAS COMPANY are prepared to SELL or HIRE GAS STOVES for Cooking and Heating purposes.

Various sizes and descriptions may be seen, and further particulars obtained, at No. 20, Vinicombe Street (corner of Byres Road), Hillhead.

GLASGOW HERALD *15 May 1885.*

———————— * ————————

I was visiting at a house lately where they performed the most wonderful culinary feats with the aid of a gas oven. This oven stands in the kitchen beside the stove, and is connected by pipes with the meter. It is quite an ornamental affair, and admirably adapted for all kinds of cookery. Indeed, my friends tell me that many people who possess those gas ovens dispense at times with their coal fire altogether, and depend upon this oven for all the boiling, stewing, roasting, and brandering — as we call it, or broiling, as English people name it — required for the household. But it is in the management of cakes and fancy bread that this gas oven particularly shines. With them it is positively irresistible, and very strangely constituted indeed, must be the preparation which could resist its kindly influence. The gas is turned on, and the oven quickly heated to the very nicest point of perfection, then the cake, or whatever else it is, is placed in it, and the same equable heat maintained until the delicious sweet-smelling compound is done to a turn! The heat of the oven being so easily regulated by the screwing off or on of the gas, and the possession of one enabling the occupier of a flat to manage during the heat of summer — (we used to have summer weather) — without that, I had almost said infernal machine, otherwise the kitchen stove, should make the gas ovens very popular.

Then the cost of a gas oven need not be an obstacle in the way of an intending purchaser, as the one my friends have got, just cost about fifty shillings; and when one thinks how servants, as a rule waste coals when no cooking is going on, another advantage of the gas oven rises alluringly before our mental vision. . . .

QUIZ *18 June 1886.*

UTILITARIAN STREET LAMPS IN GLASGOW

After much discussion, extending over several months the Watching and Lighting Committee have accepted the offer of the Pluto Company to erect at their own expense six of their lamps in various parts of the city, for the purpose of automatically supplying hot water, tea, coffee, &c., on the penny-in-the-slot principle. The sites selected are:— Bridgeton Cross, Infirmary (*Cathedral*) Square, the Phoenix Recreation Ground, Anderston Cross, Paisley Road at Morrison Street, and Rutherglen Road at Govan (*Ballater*) Street. EVENING TIMES *30 March 1899.*

A tea and coffee lamp.

TRANSPORT

After Shanks's pony, the horse formed the chief means of locomotion for many centuries, continuing as an integral part of the 18th-century canal system, and also as the source of power on the earliest railways. The spectacular multi-coloured balloons were only expensive gimmicks and could hardly be taken seriously as a mode of transport. Sedan chairs were certainly more dignified as long as nobody was in a hurry, but could hardly be considered suitable for long distances. The new level, surfaced, turnpike roads of the later 18th century provided a network for the horse-drawn stage-coaches which began to run to regular timetables. The idea of replacing them with steam-powered coaches, in 1834, was an ambitious one, but, unfortunately, doomed to failure when one blew up only four months after they had begun a regular run.

The first railway to come into the city was the Garnkirk and Glasgow, (note the order of importance!) and it was the first also to employ steam locomotives instead of horses. Its success encouraged the building of the later lines to Greenock, Ayr, and Edinburgh. It is interesting to see how the Edinburgh and Glasgow Railway Company cleverly turned the serious handicap of the long tunnel into Queen Street Station into a tourist attraction! Of course it was whitewashed in those days!! The first of the low-level railways was also at Queen Street forty years later. The newly modernised subway (or Underground as Glaswegians prefer to call it) originated with a cable system in the 1890s — a remarkably far-sighted enterprise which has only been appreciated in recent years.

———————————— * ————————————

SEDAN CHAIRS

I believe that I was present (in the hall of the old Merchants' House) at the last public ball which was given there. It was a dancing-school ball, and we all went to it in sedan chairs, through the dirty Bridgegate. These chairs were far from being comfortable conveyances, for when the chairmen were in a haste to overtake several engagements, they set off with their load at a round plunging trot, and as the carrying shafts were quite flexible and pliant, the

Sedan chairs were far from being comfortable conveyances.

extreme bobbing up and down, and swinging to and fro of the vehicle, caused by the chairmen being obliged mutually to keep the regular step, gave one the uneasy feeling of what Sir Walter Scott called a *whummle*. I cannot fix upon the exact year when the said ball took place, but think that it must have been in 1781 or 1782. The Tontine Assembly Rooms were then just opened, and after this time, the "Briggate Ha'", as it was called, was deserted as a place of public amusement.

GLASGOW PAST AND PRESENT *vol. II page 120.*

———————— * ————————

⁊ Every chairman carrying or resting his chair under cloud of night, and not having a light fixed on the fore part of one of the poles, or carrying or resting a chair on the side pavement or plain stones, shall forfeit 2s. 6d. sterling for each transgression, be imprisoned and the chair detained till the same is paid, excepting where the chairmen have occasion to use the light in going into a closs or stair for the person they are to carry, in which cases they shall have a person to take charge of the chair in their absence, under the said penalty.

2. That a number shall be distinctly painted on the front and back of each chair for hire, and that there shall not be the same number on two chairs, under the penalty of 10s. sterling for each transgression, to be paid by the owner or proprietor of the chair.

3. Any chairmasters, or persons having at the time the charge of chairs, refusing to take a fare when offered, shall be committed to prison for 24 hours, and the master and owner shall be liable in a penalty of 5s. sterling, unless he can show and prove a sufficient cause for such refusal, such as a previous engagement at that time, or any other reason to be sustained by the magistrate.

4. All masters or owners of chairs, or their servants, engaging to call for and take up any person at a particular hour, and neglecting to do so, shall be fined in 5s. sterling.

5. All masters, or owners of chairs, or their servants, demanding or asking more fare than what is established by the following table, or not having a printed copy thereof and of these regulations ready to be shown the person employing them, shall forfeit 2s. 6d. for every such offence, and likewise the hire.

6. When a number of chairmen attend at the entry to any place of public amusement, those whose chairs are not engaged shall range themselves next to the entry, but those whose chairs are engaged shall be ranged in a separate station at a convenient distance from the entry, and when any of these last are called upon by any to whom they are engaged, the chairs stationed next to the entry shall give free access to the engaged chairs. Any who shall transgress this regulation shall incur a fine of 5s. sterling.

Fees for sedan chairs:— Every lift of a sedan chair in town, though for ever so short a distance, 6d.; . . . from St. Andrew's Square to the new town, or any part of Argyle Street, and to the streets running southwards and northwards of Trongate and Argyle Street, and to St. Enoch's Square, 9d.; from the Saltmarket, Bridgegate, Clyde Street, Broomielaw and westward of Jamaica Street to Grahamston, to any part in the new town, 1s.; . . . from Gorbals to the High Church, or the like distance, 2s.; from the cross each mile round the same, 2s.; for every hour a chair waits, unless engaged for forenoon and afternoon, besides the stated hire herein provided, for the first hour, 9d., and for every subsequent hour, 6d.; for each mile

carrying to or from the city of Glasgow, 2s.; for every lift after 1 o'clock in the morning, double hire, excepting on Assembly nights; every double lift to pay double hire; two children, each not exceeding 13 years old, or one child in a person's arms, being always excepted and considered only as one lift. Every person engaging a chair and not using it, to be liable for the disappointment, 6d. . . .
EXTRACTS FROM THE BURGH RECORDS *1 March 1798.*

In the year 1800 there were 27 sedan chairs lent out to hire in this city; the number is now (1819) reduced to 18, and there is only one lady in town who keeps a sedan for her own use.
THE RISE AND PROGRESS OF THE CITY OF GLASGOW. *Cleland; 1820. page 174.*

———————— * ————————

The Monkland Canal is now finished to Glasgow, and on Monday last, the first boat with coals arrived at the bason at Howgate head; which will greatly lower the price of coals there.
EDINBURGH ADVERTISER *15 October 1784.*

———————— * ————————

BALLOONING

GRAND AIR-BALLOON

Mr. LUNARDI most respectfully informs the Public of Glasgow, Paisley, and the environs, that his intention is to gratify their curiosity, by ascending from a conspicuous place in this city. As an undertaking of this kind is attended with great expence, he has been advised by his friends to open a subscription to defray it.

Those who are disposed to honour Mr. LUNARDI with their encouragement, will be pleased to mark their names, and the sum which they intend to give, on books which are opened at the following places:

Tontine Coffee-room — Black Bull Inn — and
Saracen's Head Inn, Glasgow,
And at the New Inn, Paisley.

N.B. Subscribers will receive tickets (at THREE SHILLINGS each,) in proportion to the sum they subscribe. And as soon as TWO HUNDRED POUNDS are subscribed, Mr. LUNARDI will fix the day of his ascension into the atmosphere.

On Saturday and Monday next, the *Baloon will be* exhibited at the Assembly room, full of atmospherical air, in a manner, that the company will see not only the out-side of this large vehicle, but its beautiful in-side, as it is made with 500 yards of transparent silk, green, pink, and yellow. The door will be open from ten in the morning till dark.

ADMITTANCE to the ASSEMBLY-ROOM, Ladies and Gentlemen — One Shilling, Children — Six-pence.

GLASGOW MERCURY *10 November 1785.*

AERIAL EXCURSION

IF the weather is fine, on WEDNESDAY NEXT, about twelve o'clock at noon, Mr. LUNARDI WILL ASCEND with his BALLOON into the Atmosphere, from St. Andrew's Church-Yard, Glasgow.

Mr. Lunardi begs leave to observe, that although the subscription-money does not amount as yet to one hundred pounds, he is determined to go up on that day, trusting to the Ladies and Gentlemen that the sum of two hundred pounds, before mentioned, will not be deficient.

Tickets to admit into the Church-Yard, on the day of Mr. Lunardi's ascension, are now issued at the following places, at three shillings each.

Tontine Coffee-house,
Black Bull Inn,
Saracen's Head,
Mr. Durie's White Swan
New Inn, and Saracen's Head, Paisley.

Subscribers are requested to send for their tickets. Mr. Lunardi is also happy of having in his power to acquaint the Ladies and Gentlemen, that according to their wishes, the Magistrates have granted him *the Choir of the Old Cathedral*, where, on MONDAY NEXT, from eleven to four o'clock in the afternoon, the Balloon will be suspended, in a floating state, with the netting over it, and the car attached to it, which will be an exact representation of its ascent.

Amittance in the Choir of the Old Cathedral

ONE SHILLING.

N.B. All those who have tickets for the day of ascension, will be admitted gratis once, on shewing the ticket.

GLASGOW MERCURY *17 November 1785.*

———————— * ————————

Yesterday Mr. Lunardi, according to appointment, made his aerial expedition from St. Andrew's Church-yard. In the morning a flag was displayed from the steeple of the town-house to announce his intention of fulfilling his engagements with the public. The day proved very fine for this season, and about a quarter before two in the afternoon, the balloon being completely inflated, the adventurous aeronaut took his place in the car, and taking farewell of his friends, ascended into the atmosphere with majestic grandeur, to the astonishment and admiration of an immense crowd of spectators. It rose almost perpendicular to a great height, but not with that velocity as satisfied the adventurer, for on throwing out some ballast, its motion became very rapid, ascending in a S.E. direction and continued to be seen for about fourteen minutes. When he was at a great height, the flag was observed to drop below the car, which created a general concern among the spectators, as they apprehended the car had broke from the balloon. It is impossible to give an exact account of the number of people, of all ranks, assembled on this occasion; but we may safely say it was by far the greatest multitude ever convened in Glasgow. About two o'clock he was seen passing over Hamilton, upon which the Magistrates of that place set the bells a-ringing. It is conjectured his descent may be in the neighbourhood of Lanark or Douglas-Mill. (*He actually came down at Hawick.*)

Mr. Lunardi's aerial excursion yesterday having induced many of the neighbouring gentry to come to town, there were Rooms in the evening. The company was numerous and elegant. Mr. Lunardi is expected at the Rooms this evening.

GLASGOW MERCURY *24 November 1785.*

———————— * ————————

It gives us great pleasure to see the cutting of the Glasgow, Paisley, and Ardrossan Canal now going on vigorously within two miles of this city. This is a *Barge Canal*, the first in Scotland, on the plan of those inland navigations which, in the Manufacturing Counties in England, have been productive of immense advantages to the Country, and to Canal Proprietors.

GLASGOW HERALD *25 May 1807.*

STEAM CARRIAGES

Mr. Russell's Steam Carriages. — We noticed in our last the arrival, from Edinburgh of one of the Steam Carriages belonging to the Steam Carriage Company of Scotland. Since that time another has arrived, and they have had two or three short runs in the vicinity of the Station-house in George Square. On Saturday, at three o'clock, one of them, after going round the Square, went out three miles on the Paisley Road, and returned. The trip was not intended to shew the speed of the vehicle, but to prove the facility and safety with which it could move along our crowded streets; and that no danger whatever was to be apprehended from horses starting or shying as it passed along. On this occasion, a groom mounted on a spirited horse went alongside the whole way without its evincing the slightest symptom of alarm, and no other animal on the road took the least notice of the carriage, which made very little noise indeed. The coaches are all highly-finished, and most comfortably fitted up in the inside. A little steam is emitted at starting — but of course, there is no smoke, the fuel used being charred coke. It will be seen by an advertisement in another column that they commence running today between Paisley and this city.

GLASGOW HERALD *31 March 1834.*

THE STEAM CARRIAGE COMPANY OF SCOTLAND'S STEAM CARRIAGES

WILL RUN from their OFFICE, GEORGE'S SQUARE, between GLASGOW AND PAISLEY,

On FRIDAY and SATURDAY the 4th and 5th April, at the following hours, viz:—

From GLASGOW	From PAISLEY
At 10 o'clock, A.M.	At 12 o'clock, Noon
At 12 o'clock, Noon	At 2 o'clock, Afternoon
At 2 o'clock, Afternoon	At 4 o'clock, Afternoon
At 4 o'clock, Afternoon	At 6 o'clock, Afternoon

FARES — 2s. Inside; 1s.6d. Outside; 1s. Curricle.

Passengers may be Booked at the Company's Office, George's Square; and at the Tontine Inn, Paisley.

GLASGOW COURIER *3 April 1834.*

... they have been found to be wholly unable, as yet, to go more than five or six miles an hour. — This is the more to be regretted as it is said the company have seven or eight of these carriages, each of which cost about £700, lying finished in Edinburgh. The machinery, too, has gone out of order on one or two occasions, and on Tuesday afternoon, owing to a casualty of this kind, the coach which left Paisley at four o'clock was three or four hours on the road. . . .

GLASGOW HERALD 4 April 1834.

---- * ----

DREADFUL STEAM-CARRIAGE ACCIDENT

On Tuesday afternoon, this city was thrown into an indescribable state of excitement and alarm in consequence of the reports which reached town announcing the total destruction of one of the steam-carriages, which left Glasgow at two o'clock, on the Paisley Road, in the immediate vicinity of the Three-Mile-House. It appears that the carriage, having gained the summit of the acclivity at the place in question, stopped for a minute or two to take in a supply of fuel and water, when, just as it was in the act of proceeding on its journey, one of the right-hand wheels gave way — the machine came to the ground with terrible violence — the boiler was instantly crushed as flat as a pancake, and simultaneously with which, the bottom of the vehicle was shattered to atoms by the explosion, and all the passengers, twelve in number, were more or less injured. . . .

The noise occasioned by the explosion was so loud, that the report was distinctly heard at a distance of nearly two miles from the spot; and with such force did the steam rush out of the boiler, that the burning cinders in the furnace, together with the metal on the road, were blown to a considerable distance from the scene of the accident. So great was the explosion, that one of the windows of the Three-Mile-House was completely cleared of glass, which was shivered to atoms — an eight-day clock was also considerably damaged, and a bed in one of the back-rooms was ignited, but, luckily, the flames were speedily extinguished. A number of individuals passing on the road at the time were slightly injured by the burning cinders, stones, &c., which were scattered about in all directions to a considerable distance; and the woman of the house likewise sustained some injury from the scalding element. What was singular, the engineer, who was placed behind the carriage, and five men who were seated on the curricle, fortunately escaped unhurt. It is impossible to give any adequate idea of the sensation produced in the public mind by this untoward occurrence, or to describe the state of those parties who witnessed the deplorable accident. During the whole of the afternoon, the road was crowded with noddies, gigs, &c., with parties making anxious inquiries after the ill-starred sufferers; and it is but justice to mention, that the attention of Mr. Russell, the inventor of the carriages, who was almost instantly present with medical assistance, was conspicuous during the whole evening.

Every thing which human sympathy or medical ingenuity could suggest as calculated to alleviate the excruciating pains of the wounded, was promptly put into practice — there being no fewer than fourteen eminent surgeons present during the greater part of the afternoon. Every accommodation was freely afforded by the resident families, and it is only to be hoped that the result in various cases will not be so melancholy as was at first anticipated. Great crowds have visited the scene of the accident, and the excitement still continues. . . .

We understand that on Wednesday the Sheriff of the County, along with the Procurator Fiscal, and Bailie Stewart, instituted a judicial investigation into the circumstances and causes of the accident, by examining those who had witnessed the accident, and who had visited the ground immediately afterwards. The particulars of their enquiry have not yet reached us, but we understand the sum of evidence to be, that the accident was entirely owing to the breaking of one of the wheels, in consequence of which the whole weight fell down upon a part of the boiler, which was consequently pressed flat, and burst, and that the passengers were chiefly injured by their falling from, or leaping off, the vehicle.

GLASGOW HERALD 1 *August 1834.*

———————— * ————————

RAILWAYS

We are happy to learn that at a late meeting the Garnkirk and Glasgow Railway Company contracted with the Bedlington Iron Company for the supply of Birkinshon's Patent malleable Iron Rails, each fifteen feet long and weighing 28 lbs per lineal yard. The railway will thus be sufficient for locomotive engines, which, it is understood, will perform the haulage at fully fifty per cent less than animal power; and the road as now marked out is said to be very suitable, both in line and levels, for their use. This City, which set the example in Europe of propelling vessels in water by steam, will thus be the first to shew in Scotland the application of the same power to land carriages. The Directors have also just contracted with Messrs McCulloch & Co. of Glasgow for a large supply of cast-iron chains, with Mr. Keith of Dundee for sleepers, and likewise with Messrs. Forbes and Sutherland of Edinburgh for the execution of the earth-work on the eastern division of the line. The last of these contracts will alone give employment to about 500 men for the next 18 months. Intelligence of this kind, we are persuaded, must be peculiarly gratifying to all classes of our fellow citizens, and we have no doubt the subscribers will be amply remunerated by the traffic which such an undertaking must command. We are also informed that operations commence on Tuesday next, on which joyful occasion most of the subscribers to this magnificent undertaking have resolved to dine together in the Tontine Hotel.

GLASGOW HERALD *24 August 1827.*

---------------------- * ----------------------

GARNKIRK AND GLASGOW RAILWAY

The commencement of this great and important undertaking, which we had the gratification to announce in a late number of our paper, has now been realised; the contractors having broken ground at an early hour on Tuesday morning, in presence of several directors and spectators. In the afternoon the Company entertained a number of their friends, and gentlemen connected with the prosperity of this part of the country, at dinner, in the tontine — Mr. Dunlop of Keppoch in the chair, and Professor Jeffray of Cardowan croupier; and many loyal and appropriate toasts were drunk in the course of the evening. The commencement of this undertaking, which has for its primary object the reduction of the expense of transit of an article so essential to our manufactories as fuel, and in other respects so pre-eminently calculated to facilitate commercial intercourse, must be gratifying intelligence to all classes of our fellow citizens; for, as *steam navigation*, *manufactories*, and *population* increase, the necessity of competition and other means of conveyance become more and more obvious.

This Railway is intended to form a more direct and perfect communication with the Monkland Coal-field and this city than any hitherto executed; more particularly that extensive and valuable part of the Coalfield not immediately interesected by the Monkland Canal. . . .

In addition to the conveyance of coal, freestone and whinstone, from the various quarries situated on the Ballochney Railway, limestone from Garnkirk to the Monkland district, agricultural produce, manure, merchandise, etc., coaches for the conveyance of passengers will be established; and from the success of similar carriages lately established on the Stockton and Darlington Railway, the company are sanguine of success: on the Darlington Railway passengers are conveyed at the rate of 1d. per mile outside, and 1½d., inside, with a speed varying from 8 to 14 miles an hour; these coaches are not even placed on *springs*, yet the motion is much more easy and pleasant than can well be conceived by those who have not

Garnkirk and Glasgow Railway
STEAM CARRIAGES.
1837

Summer Hours—From 1st March to 1st November.

Glasgow to Gartsherrie Inn and Airdrie, 5½, a. m. 7¼, a. m. 11, a. m.
2, p. m. and 5, p. m.

Airdrie to Glasgow, 8½, a. m. 12, noon, 3, p. m. and 6, p. m.

Gartsherrie Inn to Glasgow, 9, a. m. 12½, p. m. 3½, p. m. and 6½, p. m.

Winter Hours—From 2d November till 28th February.

Glasgow to Gartsherrie Inn and Airdrie, 5½, a. m. 7¼, a. m. 11, a. m.
2, p. m. 4, p. m.

Airdrie to Glasgow, 8½, a. m. 12, noon, 2¼, p. m. 5, p. m.

Gartsherrie Inn to Glasgow, 9, a. m. 12½, p. m. 2¼, p. m. 5½, p. m.

Railway Depôt, 20 minutes' walk from the Cross, Glasgow.

Travellers leaving Glasgow, by the Railway Carriages, arrive at Gartsherrie Inn, 9 miles from town, in about half-an-hour. An hour generally elapses before the Carriages start on their return; and the whole excursion occupies only two hours between the time of leaving and returning to the Railway Depôt.

The time taken between Glasgow and Airdrie is about an hour.

Travellers must take charge of their own Luggage. All Luggage exceeding, in weight or bulk, what can be carried in the hand, and put under the passenger's seat, must be paid for. Dogs charged extra, and only carried when there is a spare Waggon in the Train. Smoking in the Carriages prohibited.

An Omnibus runs from Wylie & Lochhead's, 164, Trongate, to the Railway Depôt, 20 minutes before the time of starting of the Steam Carriages, and returns on their arrival.

---

experienced it. When it is considered that one horse can with ease draw one of these coaches carrying from 30 to 40 passengers, it must be obvious that even these low rates will not only afford an ample remuneration to the coach proprietors, but a considerable sum to the proprietors of the Railway.

Hitherto steam has not been applied to the haulage of Railway carriages in this part of the island, although it has been in use for some years past in several parts of England; and it is obvious, as these machines and roads are improved in their construction, their superiority over animal power will be fully ascertained. As this

Railway, both in line and level, is extremely suitable for their application, it is the intention of the Company to use these machines as soon as the embankments are sufficiently consolidated. We therefore look forward with much interest to the completion of this Railway, as affording an application of steam to which we have hitherto been unaccustomed.

GLASGOW HERALD 31 August 1827.

———————— * ————————

THE QUEEN STREET STATION TUNNEL

On Thursday evening we had the pleasure of inspecting the Tunnel at the Glasgow terminus of the Edinburgh and Glasgow Railway, and of observing the effect of its being lighted up for the first time with gas. The excavation extends for 1250 yards, nearly three-quarters of a mile, and is lighted up by 43 lamps, distant about 80 feet from each other, the lamps being placed alternately on the east and west sides of the Tunnel. The lights are afforded by the fan-tail burners originally introduced by Mr. Neilson of the Gas Works; and, being enclosed in large semi-hexagonal lanterns, with a slightly curved reflector, throws a brilliant light over the breadth of the line, and displays to much advantage the whole interior of the vast, and admirably executed undertaking. As the lamps will be kept burning night and day, during the running of the various trains, the dull, cheerless, and to many, alarming feeling, which passing through a dark tunnel usually excites, will be entirely removed, the effect being little else than the ordinary passage through a somewhat narrow street. . . .

The Tunnel is entirely white-washed throughout, and presents a very splendid appearance, while it creates a feeling of the utmost security, although the spectator is conscious of the immense superincumbent masses of rock and other strata, which are resting above him. In one or two places only is the dropping of water to be detected, and these portions have been covered over with sheet lead, by which the water is conveyed to each side of the archway, and received in gutters, by which means the roadway is kept dry, and the feeling of comfort unaffected. The immense passenger shed was also lighted up on Thursday evening for the first time, and had a noble appearance, the ranges of lamps on each side spreading a blaze of light over the whole area, while in approaching the terminus through the Tunnel the effect of the shed lights is very striking. We observe that, today, and for one or two days in the beginning of the week, the Tunnel is to be opened for the inspection of the public, at a very moderate charge, the proceeds to be equally divided between the Paisley Fund for the relief of the unemployed, and the relief of the families of those who have been hurt or killed during the progress of the works. We doubt not that a vast concourse of persons will, especially during the holidays, be anxious to have a view of the stupendous undertaking, more particularly, as after the Railway is opened the opportunities of careful inspection will be almost entirely at an end. . . .

GLASGOW CONSTITUTIONAL *1 January 1842.*

———————————— * ————————————

CHEAP EXCURSIONS

For the Fast-Day, the Glasgow and South-Western Railway Company announce special cheap excursions over the greater part of their line at single fare for the double journey, and they run a special train to the Ayrshire Coast at an even greater reduction.

The Caledonian Railway Company allow the same liberal facilities, and also advertise such cheap runs as to Oban and back for 5s.

QUIZ *26 October 1883.*

GLASGOW, PAISLEY, KILMARNOCK AND AYR RAILWAY.

SUMMER ARRANGEMENTS.
1844

On MONDAY, 1st MAY, and until farther Notice, the following TRAINS will be Run:—

FROM GLASGOW TO KILMARNOCK, AYR, &c.

† At 6 Morning.	At Half-past 1 Afternoon.
* Half-past 7 do.	§ Half-past 4 do.
Half-past 10 do.	* Half-past 6 Evening.

† This Train goes to Kilmarnock only, in connection with the Standard Coach to Dumfries, Carlisle, &c.

FROM AYR *To Glasgow, Kilmarnock, &c.*	FROM KILMARNOCK *To Glasgow, Ayr, &c.*
* At 8 Morning.	* At 20 Min. past 8 Morning.
11 Forenoon.	§ 20 Min. past 11 Forenoon.
2 Afternoon.	20 Min. past 2 Afternoon.
5 do.	20 Min. past 5 do.
* 7 Evening.	* 20 Min. past 7 Evening.

No Trains on Sunday.

QUEEN STREET LOW LEVEL RAILWAY

Last week I was permitted to visit this great railway undertaking which is being quietly constructed underneath our houses. The shaft through which I descended was 100 feet in depth, and the sensation which one feels in going so deeply into the bowels of the earth is certainly worth experiencing. About a third of the work is done, and the circular route from Stobcross to High Street is expected to be completed in about two years. One thousand navvies are employed on the railway.

QUIZ 18 April 1884.

———————— * ————————

THE CATHCART RAILWAY

The Cathcart District Railway has been fairly on its trial since it opened on the 1st. inst., and, as usual, there has been no lack of the grumblers who, on such an occasion, are always to the fore with suggestions — some of them bordering on demands — that the Caledonian Railway, who, of course, know nothing about their own business, should frame a time-table and tariff of fares to suit their (the grumblers') individual convenience and purses.

In the interests of my readers, I have had a run on the line. My experience and that of a number of regular travellers to whom I have spoken go to prove that this new means of egress from the murky city to the breezy suburbs of Pollokshields, Crosshill, and Mount Florida, not to mention that most bracing of the lungs of the city, the Queen's Park, is a great boon to our South-Side "barnacles". All that is wanted to secure success is punctuality; and, with a little experience, the congestion caused by the arrival or despatch of sixty-four additional trains daily at the Central Station will, I make no doubt, get relieved, and the irregularities which have occasionally been manifest will disappear.

The grumblers who take exception to the nomenclature of the stations at Crosshill appear to me, however, to have the right end of the stick. "Queen's Park" should certainly have been "Crosshill", and "Crosshill" "Myrtle Park".

QUIZ 12 March 1886.

———————— * ————————

GLASGOW DISTRICT SUBWAY

After six years have been spent in its construction, in the course of which many difficulties have been overcome, the Glasgow District Subway is practically completed. Apart from the fact that it will provide a cheap and easy means of access to a large part of the city,and provide facilities for travelling between parts on opposite sides of the river, which at present can only be reached in a round-about way, the Subway has several unique features which make it worthy of a city spoken of as the pioneer municipality in the world. To begin with, it is the first underground passenger railway in the world to adopt cable haulage. All the others are tramways or railways running along a street, where the progress of the cars is interfered with by other vehicular traffic and the speed correspondingly limited. Thirdly, it is the first cable railway with a circular route.

The bill authorising the construction of the subway was passed in 1890, and in the autumn of that year the actual work of construction began. Roughly speaking, the subway has cost £1,000,000 to make, including the amount expended in tunnelling, laying the permanent way, and providing cables, machinery, cars, and station buildings. In addition, the promoters had to expend a large sum on the purchase of property, as only a small part of the line runs underneath the centre of streets. . . . Slightly elliptical in form, and entirely underground, the subway is 6½ miles in length, and is so cosmopolitan in its character as to embrace the business centre of the city, the better class residential districts, the localities where our industrious artizans dwell, and the docks and shipbuilding yards where they earn their daily bread. All sections of the community, especially those who work or dwell in the western part of the city, on either side of the river, will find in the subway an important addition to the existing means of transit. . . . There are 15 stations situated less than half a mile from each other. . . .

The subway consists throughout of two sets of rails, each running in a separate tunnel 11 feet in internal diameter. The top of the tunnels varies in depth beneath the surface of the ground, from 20 feet at Govan, to 122 feet in Hillhead. In the northern and western districts a great deal of hard rock had to be bored, but the greatest difficulties were encountered in low-lying grounds adjoining and beneath the Clyde, where mud and shifting sand had to be dealt with. Messrs. Simpson and Wilson, the well-known Glasgow firm, who are the engineers of the subway, adopted the compressed air system of excavating in these parts of the tunnels, the interiors being lined with iron built up in segments as the digging proceeded fitting water tight. This, though obviating the opening of the ground along the entire length of the subway as was done in constructing of the Central Railway beneath Argyll Street, was a very costly undertaking. In some parts, however, it was found possible to work on the cut and cover system — that is excavating from the surface downward, building the concrete arch, and then removing the soil from underneath. At each of the stations a single arch, with a span of 28 feet, covers both tracks, which run alongside an island platform, 10 feet wide and an average of 150 feet in length. At Buchanan Street Station the platform is 40 feet below the surface of the street, which is the greatest depth of any of the platforms. In the opposite extreme the platform of Kinning Park Station is only 14 feet below the street. . . . The platforms are reached by staircases from 6 to 8 feet wide. At the top of these are turnstiles, at which passengers will pay the penny which will carry them to any station.

There are two cables for hauling the cars, each cable going round the entire circle in one direction, while that on the other track goes round in the opposite direction. Thus, in case of a breakdown on one of the lines, the other rope will still run, so that only one set of cars will be stopped instead of both, as would have been the case, had the rope been worked on the system which is usual on cable tramways. It may be mentioned that besides the two cables which are running, there are other two kept in reserve. Each cable weighs 57 tons, and costs from £1,600 to £2,000. The gauge of the railway is 4 feet, instead of the standard 4ft. 8½ in., the object being to secure a better permanent way by removing the rails further from the sides of the tunnel. The cables will run on the usual sheaves, and be two inches or so above the level of the rails. At the outset it is intended to run the cable at a speed of 15 miles an hour. . . .

Each car is 41 feet in length over the platform, while the body of the car is 32 feet. Each is mounted on two bogies, so that there are eight wheels. Nominally, they are each seated for 42 passengers, but their breadth, which is a foot more than that of the Corporation tramway cars, will allow additional passengers to stand in the centre without causing inconvenience to the sitters. When empty, each car weighs seven tons, while with all the seats occupied the weight will be ten tons. Each train will consist of two cars placed with their doors facing each other. One of the cars will be for smokers, the other for non-smokers. . . . Passengers will have little time to wait, as there will be to all intents and purposes a continuous service from about five in the morning till shortly after eleven o'clock at night. When work ends for the day the cars will remain overnight at the stopping station. The cars will be lit by electricity on the trolley system, a wheel on the side of the cars running on a rail fixed to the side of the tunnel. The stations and other buildings will also be lit by electricity. As there will be neither smoke, steam, nor other vapour, the air in the tunnels will be pure, and there is no necessity for ventilating shafts.

EVENING TIMES *10 September 1896.*

AMUSEMENTS

A fashionable Dancing Assembly in 1825.

We think of the Georgian period as one of taste and elegance. It was, of course, in the upper classes of society with their fashionable dresses and dancing Assemblies, but there was a darker side to life as well. It was really rather a callous age. One can glimpse this in the too-frequent appearances of unhappy, deformed people, exhibited as freaks — objects of vulgar curiosity rather than pity. The success of these shows seems to have been in proportion to their capacity to make the spectator feel comfortably superior. The 19th century brought with it the benefits of gas lighting, although it was not without its drawbacks as was demonstrated by the burning of the Queen Street Theatre Royal eleven years after it had adopted the new form of illumination. In considering one of the advertisements for that theatre, for Mozart's *Marriage of Figaro*, in 1828, one wonders what he would have thought of his masterpiece being interspersed with "favourite Scotch songs"!

With the passing of the years the amusements became gradually more sophisticated, the human exhibits largely replaced by animals. Circuses were in great demand. The Victorians enthusiastically attended any entertainment which promised to lift them out of their endlessly humdrum existence. The firework display at Cranstonhill and the magic of the Wizard of the North, paved the way for the most lasting of these, the Victorian pantomime which reached its high point in the 1870s and 1880s. An entertainingly detailed account of a visit to Glasgow Fair in 1864 forms an appropriate centrepiece for this motley collection.

------------------ * ------------------

NO ENTERTAINMENTS IN
THE GRAMMAR SCHOOL

The magistrats and toun councill, considering that the allowing of publick balls, shows, comedies and other plays or diversions, where acted in houses belonging to the town, and particularly in the Gramar Schooll house, hes occasioned great disturbance in the citie, do therefor strictly prohibit and discharge the allowing of publik balls, shews, comedies and other plays and diversions to be acted or done within any of the touns houses, and particularly within the Gramar Schooll, excepting such plays as are acted by the boys of the schooll, and have relation to their learning and to be acted by none else but themselves, and none others to be present thereat but the masters and schollars of the school, and remit to the magistrats to see that this act be not contraveened.

EXTRACTS FROM THE BURGH RECORDS *20 February 1721*.

------------------ * ------------------

ASSEMBLIES

Glasgow Mercury, 27th January 1780. The Dancing Assemblies are to be carried on this year by a General Subscription, it being found of late that the money taken at the door will not answer the expense. They are to be held regularly at the *Rooms* on Tuesday evenings once a fortnight during the season.

A book is opened, where Gentlemen may subscribe, at One Guinea each for the season, and lies for that purpose at Messrs. Campbell and Ingram's Insurance Office.

The ladies are to pay nothing.

Stranger Gentlemen will be admitted on paying 2s 6d at the door of the room. No town's gentlemen will be admitted but subscribers.

There will be a Dancing Assembly on Tuesday the 1st of February, to begin precisely at six o'clock.

N.B. There will be Card Assemblies every alternate Tuesday evening, on the usual footing.

From the above advertisement it will be seen that the aristocratic directors of these assemblies kept the freedom of admission to the said assemblies in their own hands, in so far as concerned Glasgow gentlemen. This was done for the purpose of excluding the *shopocracy* of the city from mixing in the country dances with the wives and daughters of the great Virginian merchants.

GLASGOW PAST AND PRESENT *vol. III page 343.*

To all who are admirers of Extraordinary Productions of Nature

Just arrived, and to be seen by any number of persons, in Mr. BROWN'S Auction-Room, near the head of the Saltmarket, from eleven in the morning, till nine in the evening,

THE SURPRISING DWARF

He is twenty-three years of age,
and not thirty-one inches high.

His surprising smallness makes a striking impression, at first sight, on the spectator's mind. His countenance and figure are extremely agreeable, and his manner and address give general satisfaction.

N.B. He is the shortest person that has ever been exhibited to the Public.

ALSO
A YOUNG LADY
FROM NEWFOUNDLAND
BORN WITHOUT ARMS

This curious phenomenon of nature, without hands, cuts watch papers with her toes in the neatest manner, and presents them to Gentlemen and Ladies; threads the finest needle; does any part of needle-work, and marks initial letters on linen to great perfection.

Admittance to Ladies and Gentlemen
ONE SHILLING
Tradesmen and Children SIX-PENCE.

I attended this exhibition, but . . . I felt greatly disappointed at the sight of the dwarf mentioned in the above advertisement. He had nothing manly in his appearance; on the contrary, he seemed like a child dressed up with the habiliments of a full-grown man. His features were soft, and his manners, though good, could easily have been taught to a clever child: in short, many of the visitors doubted his age being 23, as stated by him, and suspected that he was not the one half of that period of life, and that, in fact, he was only a smart child, possessing the countenance and manners of a grown-up person. The public therefore felt little interest as to this dwarf, but they showed great curiosity in regard to the lady born without arms, whose wonderful dexterity in the use of her toes caused not only great astonishment but much merriment to the beholders. . . . She sat upon a cushion, with her feet bare; and it was truly surprising to see with what ease she used her toes in threading a needle, in hemming handkerchiefs, in embroidering, and in doing other feats of needlework. She was equally skilful in the management of her scissors and the use of her pen. I had the honour of receiving a watch-paper from this lady, neatly cut out by her with scissors.

GLASGOW PAST AND PRESENT *vol. III page 338.*

———————— * ————————

. . . Let us here take a vivid peep at the old magnificent Theatre Royal in Queen Street (afterwards burned to the ground), as we remember it on the first grand and important occasion when it was to be lighted up with gas to the view of the excited citizens. Mr. John Corri, as he was called, had just arrived in the city from London, with his signors and signoras, and had advertised in the newspapers the performance of Mozart's grand operas of Giovanni and Figaro for Friday, the 18th of September, 1818, on which occasion the grand crystal lustre from the roof of the Theatre, the largest of any at that time in Scotland — would, in place of the wicks, and the candles, and the oil lamps, be *"illuminated with sparkling gas"*. Every seat in the boxes, up to the double and triple tiers, had been anxiously pre-engaged; the spacious pit was crammed almost to suffocation; and the first, second, and third galleries, for there were also *three* of them, had not an inch of standing room to spare, so great was the crowd, and the eager desire to gain admission, — not so much for the *music*, delightful though it was, as to behold for the first time the wonderful evolutions of the *gas*, never till then seen or heard of in any theatre in this kingdom. Nearly all the rank, wealth, and beauty of the city appeared in full dress, and were seated there. The magnates of the College — including Professors Davidson, Young, and Mylnes, with their smiling wives and beautiful daughters, — the Grahams, the Buchanans, the Maxwells, the Stirlings, the Dennistouns, the Tennents, the Hamiltons, the Monteiths, &c.,&c. But, conspicuous amongst them all, were two of the greatest beauties that probably ever shone in Glasgow, acknowledged on all hands to be "the loveliest of the lovely". The very gods in the galleries started from their seats, and greeted them with hearty cheers and rounds of applause, for which in return they made the most bewitching smiles. We allude to the lovely Miss McLean; and to the equally lovely Miss Logan, . . . Thus assembled in that theatre, — the signal being given, and the green curtain of the stage drawn up to display the magnificent drop scene of the Clyde from Bowling to Dumbarton Castle, painted on canvas by Sir Henry Raeburn, which those who saw it, and the still few alive who may remember it, can or could only do so with a glow of admiration; but it unfortunately perished in the flames, never to be replaced by the same artist hand again, — the enrapt audience, joining in the chorus to the King's Anthem, and smiling in each other's faces, from the lustre of those lights, broke out again and again into a rapture of applause; whilst the gas, as if by *magic*, made its original evolutions to their perfect astonishment, leaving some of them to fancy that they had been ushered into a new world — a perfect Elysium on earth.

REMINISCENCES OF GLASGOW *Mackenzie. vol. II page 152.*

---

*

THE BRIDGETON TEA GARDEN

D. Hamilton begs leave to return his sincere thanks to those ladies and gentlemen who honoured him with their presence last season, and informs them that the Garden having undergone considerable improvements this spring, is now ready for the reception of Company, who can be supplied with Tea, Coffee, Strawberries and Cream, and fruits in their seasons. Also liquors of the best quality, and on the most moderate terms. The Garden is neatly fitted up with Bowers, and parties from town or country will find it a most agreeable retreat to spend an hour, as they will have liberty to walk in the Garden, which is allowed by judges to be one of the pleasantest in the neighbourhood of Glasgow.

GLASGOW HERALD *29 April 1825.*

BRIDGETON TEA GARDEN
TO LET

Entering from Main Street, with the greenhouse, Arbours, Baths, Aviary, and Fishpond, and a house consisting of four rooms, kitchen, and shop, with suitable cellars. The garden is well stocked with fruit trees and bushes, flowers and shrubs, and the rent is moderate.

GLASGOW HERALD *27 November 1826.*

HAMILTON'S OLD TEA
GARDENS,
BRIDGETON.

THOMAS MILLAR returns his most sincere thanks to his friends and the public for the liberal encouragement experienced by him since occupying the above Gardens, and takes liberty to announce that the Gardens are now in fine order, and that he continues to supply the visitors with fruits of all kinds in their season. Malt and Spirituous Liquors of every description and of the best quality.

GLASGOW HERALD *17 July 1835.*

———————— * ————————

Attempted Suicide. — On Sabbath afternoon, the visitors to the Bridgeton Tea Gardens were rather surprised, while perambulating one of the walks, to find a man suspended by the neck to one of the trees. No time was lost in cutting him down, but life to all appearance was extinct. After applying the usual means, however, he was brought to a state of animation, and with some difficulty conveyed to the Calton Police Office, where he turned out to be a William Collins, an old drummer in the army. He declared in the office that he had got himself wet with whisky, and had "hung himself up to dry," and that he would do it again. He was ordered on Monday to be taken to the Justice of Peace office.

GLASGOW HERALD *3 April 1840.*

BRIDGETON TEA GARDENS

MR. PETER HATTRICK, Herbalist, begs leave to acquaint his Friends and the Public of Glasgow and Neighbourhood, that he has OPENED these PREMISES, No. 128 Main Street, Bridgeton, formerly occupied by Mr. Arthur, and which are now fitted up in a superior style of accommodation for Parties who may honour him with a visit.

His Stock of Foreign and British Spirits, Ales, &c., will be found to be of the first Quality: also his own well known and highly appreciated Tonic Bitters. The Gardens and Booths for refreshments, will, in the course of the Winter months be, as far as possible, improved, under the direction of an experienced Gardener, and no expense will be spared in rendering them an agreeable resort as the ensuing Spring and Summer months advance.

P.H. will continue to prepare his Tonic Bitters, also Herbs and Roots of all kinds and Medicine, at his Shop, fitted up at the above Premises.

N.B. — P.H.'s Tonic Bitters, in Bottles and Packages, can be had of Mr. William Barr, Wine and Spirit Merchant, 60 Jamaica Street; and Mr. T. Sprewl, Spirit Dealer, corner of Spout Mouth, Gallowgate, both of whom are appointed Agents for the accommodation of his Customers in the City and West End.

GLASGOW HERALD *20 October 1848.*

"Parties will find it a most agreeable retreat."

[129]

A UNIQUE MARRIAGE OF FIGARO

THEATRE ROYAL, QUEEN STREET.
FOR THE BENEFIT OF MISS STEPHENS

And the Last Night of her performing; also of
MISS JOHNSON & MR. HUNT'S

Appearance this Season; on which occasion
MR. MURRAY

Manager of the Theatre Royal, Edinburgh (who has kindly offered his assistance) will appear in one of his favourite characters, positively for this evening only.

Also
MR. WEEKS.

On this Evening, FRIDAY, 25th July, his Majesty's Servants will perform the Comic Opera, called the

MARRIAGE OF FIGARO.

The character of Susanna, by Miss STEPHENS, Who will Sing during the Evening, Hurrah for the Bonnets of Blue — There's a bonny briar bush — Auld Robin Gray — I've been roaming — Coming thro' the Rye.

The Countess Almaviva, by Miss JOHNSON,
Who will sing, Come ever leave me — And Duet
with Miss STEPHENS, of "How gently."

Count Almaviva, by Mr. HUNT,
Who, during the evening, will Sing — Love has Eyes — Blue Bonnets over the Border — and with Miss STEPHENS, the Duett of "The Fairest Flower."

Figaro, . . . by Mr. MURRAY,
Who will Sing the whole of the Original Music.

To conclude with the National Melo-Drama, of
ROB ROY.
Diana Vernon, by Miss STEPHENS.
Rob Roy, . . . Mr. SEYMOUR.
Francis Osbaldistone, by Mr. HUNT.
Major Galbraith, by Mr. WEEKES,
Who will sing in the course of the evening — Katty O'Lynch — Auld Lunny Flyn.

Boxes 4s. — Pit 3s. — 1st Gal. 1s. — 2d Gal. 6d. — The second price taken at nine o'clock, Boxes 2s 6d., Pit 1s 6d., Gallery 6d.

GLASGOW HERALD 25 July 1828.

FOR A SHORT TIME ONLY

Just Arrived
AND NOW EXHIBITING AT
THE ASSEMBLY ROOMS,
INGRAM STREET.

NAPOLEON BREATHING.— The most wonderful Anatomical Figure in the World, and which has attracted the Admiration of all Scientific Men in London, Dublin, &c.

This is the most astonishing Mechanical figure ever produced, and has been designated a real phenomenon of Art and Science. It is composed of a new and artificial substance, termed "Sarkomos". It represents Napoleon reposing on a couch, clad in military costume with *his own hat and sword*; and is universally allowed to be the most perfect artificial figure ever brought before the public.

The proprietor has procured from Monsieur Anto Marchi, a Cast from the Original, taken from the head of Napoleon, at St. Helena, immediately after his death.

Admittance, 1s.; Children, 6d. Open from 11 till 6, and from 7 till 10 o'clock.

Casts sold at the rooms.

GLASGOW HERALD *18 May 1835.*

COOKE'S NEW CIRCUS,
AND EQUESTRIAN
ESTABLISHMENT,
GLASGOW GREEN.

Great Novelty, with Immense Attraction!

On MONDAY, August 3d, and the following Evenings.

MR. COOKE, anxious to place his Establishment on a higher footing than a mere vehicle of amusement, presents to the Public a *Novel and Instructive Series of Tableaux*, from the highest classical authorities, which will be represented in Dresses of such peculiar colour and make as to convey the very imposing effect of TWO MARBLE STATUES, by Messrs. W. & J. COOKE. In this attempt these Brothers have had in view the exhibition of a series of Sculptural beauties, which every lover of the Arts will recognise, and, to judge from past attempts, which every spectator of genius will approve. — This scena is represented on an elevated Pedestal; and Mr. Smith, in the character of possessor of "Lo Studio," will explain the arrangement of the subjects represented in this extraordinary Performance.

A Grand Historical Equestrian Scene, in three distinct parts, invented by Mr. JAMES COOKE, and to be enacted by him on horseback, while at full speed, representing the Shakesperian Characters of SIR JOHN FALSTAFF, SHYLOCK, IN THE TRIAL SCENE: AND RICHARD III, AT THE BATTLE OF BOSWORTH.

A Splendid Variety of other Equestrian Entertainments will be given, and which are fully detailed in hand bills.

The whole concluding with (for the first time this season,) Mr. WELL'S

ASTONISHING EQUILIBRIUMS! SURROUNDED BY A BRILLIANT DISPLAY OF FIREWORKS.

BOXES, 2s. — PIT, 1s. — GALLERY, 6d.

No Half-Price to any part of the house, excepting to the boxes, where Children under ten years of age will be admitted for One Shilling.

---

*

THE ERUPTION OF VESUVIUS

Perhaps there is no "lion" in the West which has of late excited so much interest as the Eruption of Mount Vesuvius in the Zoological Gardens at Cranstonhill. The display is a perfectly novel one in this part of the country, and on exhibition nights the grounds have been peopled by from 1500 to 4000 persons, while outside the road has been crowded as far down nearly as Partick, embracing a mass of gratis on-lookers which has been estimated at more than 40,000 in number. The crash of the eruption strikes everyone with awe and dread at the moment, and the brilliancy of the fire-works throws a flood of light over the western part of the city, and is witnessed by delighted eyes at the distance of several miles. Even by daylight the perspective of Vesuvius and the adjacent mountains affords a good treat, and we are glad to observe that the grounds are being peopled with rare birds and beasts, which must gratify not only the curious, but be the source of interest and instruction to the lovers of natural history.

GLASGOW HERALD 27 July 1840.

———————— * ————————

BOTANICAL GARDENS

New Botanic Garden. — The preparation of the ground for the new Botanic Garden is this season making great progress. A large portion of it has been laid off in walks, and the removal of trees and plants from the old to the new grounds is rapidly proceeding. The ground is beautifully undulating, completely rural, and far removed from

The Botanic Gardens —
a place of instruction and amusement.

any of the public works which in almost any other quarter would have rendered the atmosphere too impure for healthy vegetation. A due share of the ground will be reserved for greensward, which at all times has an agreeable effect. It is bounded on the north by the River Kelvin at the Pear-tree well, and on the south by the Great Western Road, the only fine approach to the city. Another excellent road has been opened up, *via* Partick, from the Garden gate to the Dumbarton Road; and a drive outwards by the one road and homewards by the other, will doubtless become a favourite recreation. The new Observatory is within a few hundred yards of the Garden, and is now finished externally. It is a plain, substantial edifice, and stands on an eminence commanding an extensive view.

GLASGOW HERALD *16 April 1841.*

---------------- * ----------------

What is to be the upshot of the Botanic Gardens muddle? I know what I would like to see. I would like the place to be leased by one of those gentlemen who cater for the New York public at Coney Island or Staten Island, and who would make it a huge display of fireworks, coloured fountains, open-air concerts, swings, hobby-horses, ball-rooms, and a half-dozen gigantic restaurants and dining and drinking places. In point of fact, I would like to see it given over to the vulgar. This city is a long way too respectable . . .

QUIZ *4 March 1887.*

---------------- * ----------------

MONTEITH ROOMS,
BUCHANAN STREET.
LAST WEEK BUT ONE, OF THE
EXTRAORDINARY
PERFORMANCES OF
PROFESSOR J. H. ANDERSON.

His Engagements in the North cause him to finish his season of Wonderworking in this City; it is not the want of patronage; the Mystic Temple is as crowded Nightly as it was the First Week! (this is the Seventh Week)!! On this Evening and every Evening during the week, he will appear in his Mystic Laboratory and perform all his startling Feats of NATURAL MAGIC, illustrative of the fallacy of

DEMONOLOGY AND
WITCHCRAFT.

For the First time he will perform a most INCREDIBLE EXPERIMENT in CONNECTION with the Medical Science,

SUSPENSION CHLOROFOREENE!!

He will introduce his Son, a Child of 5 years of age: he will Suspend him in the *Air while Asleep*, in a reclining position. This wonder of Modern Science is accomplished through the agency of

CONDENSED CHLOROFORM!

Doors Open at Half-past 7; the Professor Opens at a Quarter past 8.

GLASGOW HERALD *9 October 1848.*

———————— * ————————

Saturday night at the Theatre 1825.

GLASGOW GREEN — WHAT I SAW WHEN I WALKED THE FAIR

Glasgow Fair is evidently in the last stages of a decline. It is afflicted with old age and poverty, and the "ill-matched pair" are playing the very deuce with the time-honoured carnival. It is getting more ragged, dirty-looking, and disreputable year after year, and to all appearance the beginning of the end is at hand. The booths, as a general rule, consist of rickety erections of bare fir deals, covered with patched and rotten canvas, instead of the bright yellow-painted caravans, with their magnificent pictures of wild beasts, dwarfs, and giants that were wont to fire the youthful imaginations, and fill the heads of old and young with exaggerated ideas of the sights to be witnessed within. The jokes and wry-mouths of the Merry Andrews have at length become stale, flat, and unprofitable; the tumblers and touters are getting more hoarse and more shabby in appearance; and the brass instruments are evidently afflicted with bronchitis, and are dying for want of wind. Even Mumford's booth has cut the connection and set up in the auctioneering and book-selling business after a probationary period in the preaching and social improvement line; and the South Prison this year seems to frown more grimly than usual upon the heterogeneous collection of persons and things rejoicing in the questionable title of "The Fair". . . .

Well, the dingy-looking Saltmarket is crowded, as usual on such occasions, with a moving mass of men, women, and children, in every style of dress, but the great majority evidently belong to the poorer classes. There are stalls by the wayside, where baps, biscuits, dulce, toys, sweeties, and treacle mixtures in endless variety are exposed for sale; and there are barrows laden with nuts and "grosets" moving about and making eddies among the crowd. The square in front of the South Prison is filled to overflowing with a motley collection of sightseers, and the air is resounding with strains of music, chiefly of the earpiercing kind. There are bagpipes and bass drums, cymbals, trumpets, trombones and touting horns of all shapes and dimensions, and the medley of tunes torn and twisted out of these instruments by men and boys, almost black in the face with blowing, is positively sufficient to drive a sensitive person mad. And then the touters and tumblers, in stage dresses of many colours, soiled and threadbare, are yelping, shouting, cutting capers, and doing their very best to attract attention, and get people with pennies in their pockets to "walk up and be in time".

I enter a large wooden erection, where magic and melo-drama are the principal attractions, where tobacco-pipes are being smoked, and where lemonade and pancakes are hawked about for sale. The magic was moderately good, and after magic came tumbling, and after tumbling a melo-drama in three acts which lasted about eleven minutes and a half. The *dramatis personae* of this picture of real life, consisted of a pirate or two, a young lady in distress, a couple of British sailors, a negro, and a Newfoundland dog. The pirates, as a matter of course, are intent upon killing the sailors, carrying off the young lady, and turning the negro into cash; but the lady, with a pair of rusty pistols, rushes in and rescues the negro; and, as one good turn deserves another, the negro afterwards rushes in and rescues the young lady. But the bloodthirsty pirates return to the charge, and in turn they are charged by the sailors and the dog, when a "terrific combat" with broken swords about a foot in length ensues, and the curtain drops amid thunders of applause. We are then turned out by a side door, the stage-manager hoping all the time that we are perfectly satisfied with the performance, which of course, we are.

After the melo-dramatic performance I turn into a "Temple of the Arts", where visitors are expected to entertain themselves by looking through magnifying glasses at frozen-looking pictures in the wooden walls. Besides these interesting matters, there are a few wax figures in corners, representing a murderer and his victim, a dying soldier, Highland Jessie the heroine of Lucknow, and Tantia Topee "the Inden", with a rusty flint musket in his hand. There is nothing remarkable about this exhibition except the emptiness of the place; so I walk out again and into a caravan about ten feet square, where "the Smallest Married Man in the World" exhibits himself, and where "the dreadful flood at Sheffield has lately been added". The "dreadful flood" aforesaid is shown upon a transparent picture; and there we see numerous brick buildings standing amid the water like islands, while horses, cattle, pigs, household furniture, and helpless women and children are floating about as thick as locusts, and looking pretty comfortable, all things considered. There were many other pictures of battles, sieges, and so on, which I need not particularise; and when the exhibitor held them up separately between the paraffine lamps and the audience, they (the pictures) looked as well as could be expected, and that is not saying a great deal in their favour. But the inside of the caravan is a perfect Black Hole of Calcutta with heat and darkness, so I leave it as soon as possible, and seek the open air.

Looking to the left, I observe on a picture a couple of gigantic gorillas, fierce and formidable, defending themselves against a dozen or two of men, who are armed with bows and arrows, guns, axes, spears, and other weapons, and yet the gorillas appear to have the best of the fight. "Here," said I, "are the animals for my money!" and so saying I made the best of my way to the mouth of the gorilla's den. It was a structure composed in a great measure of old, weather-beaten canvas, and, if anything, rather tattered and torn than otherwise. The charge was only one halfpenny; and when it is considered that a "happy family" of dogs, with three and five legs, monkeys with the usual number, besides rabbits, fowls, and other creatures were to be seen, in addition to a real, *bona fide*, living gorilla, it cannot be said, with any show of reason, that the entry money was exorbitant. A flap in the canvas wall having been drawn aside, I entered, and found myself in front of a broken-down cage, the habitation of the "happy family" aforesaid; but, so far as I could judge from appearances, the happiness was more imaginary than real. There was a box in a corner of the enclosure, which was understood to be the lair of the gorilla, and after the obliging proprietor had shown us his dogs with odd numbers of legs, and a ferret from the Far East, he laid his hand upon the gorilla's box, and his features assumed rather a serious appearance. He charged the little boys in the foreground to "stand back" as the animal was sometimes quite ferocious, and might tear two or three of them in the twinkling of an eye. Of course expectation was on the tiptoe, and when a good ring was formed the exhibitor removed the lid of the box, and out came an ordinary ape. He (that is, the exhibitor) set the creature upright on the top of the box, to make it look as tall as possible, assuring the company at the same time that it was a genuine article, only eighteen months old — although its countenance looked as grizzly and grave as if it had been a grandfather in Africa in the days of Mungo Park. We were assured that, in seven years or thereabouts, it would grow to be a gorilla, the finest of its family; and with this assurance and a quiet laugh, I left the exhibition, under a pretty strong impression that I had been "taken in, and done for".

Next door to the gorilla's tabernacle was a little booth, where birds and white mice went through various performances for the benefit of "the ladies and gentlemen" who had paid their halfpennies and walked in. Those little feathered and four-footed creatures drew carriages, fired pistols, imitated Blondin on the tight rope, and, in short, exerted themselves amazingly in a variety of ways. Leaving the bird and white mice exhibition, I pushed through the crowd to a wax-work over the way, where I saw the heads of four-and-twenty murderers, all in a row, or rather a number of rows, for they were built a-top of one another like a cart-load of turnips. Then came "Daniel in the Lions' Den," with a dozen or so of fierce-looking lions for companions; and the way that these terrible animals rolled their eyes and wagged their heads and their jaws was worth all the entrance money, which, I think, was a penny. But over and above

"Daniel" and the lions and the murderers' heads, we had groups representing Napoleon's death-bed scene in the Island of St. Helena, and her Majesty the Queen surrounded by the rest of the Royal Family, including General Tom Thumb. There were other groups also, but I forget all about them, so they shall be left to the reader's imagination. It is requisite that every visitor should take his imagination along with him if he intends to study figures in wax at the Fair, for it helps to make out the likenesses wonderfully, and there is ample room in this respect for its exercise on the present occasion. The fact is, that wax is something more than plentiful at the foot of the Saltmarket at the present moment. It is almost everywhere present, and in every shape and form which fancy can desire. There are solitary figures and groups of great men and women in every style of dress and in every stage of shabbiness imaginable. There are duplicates of "Daniels" and "Queens" and "Royal Families" without the slightest resemblance to each other, or to the living or dead originals. In short, the shows are overflowing with wax, and, so far as I can judge, it is not improving in shape as it becomes more plentiful.

After a feast of figures and a flow of wax, I made my way to a little caravan, where a great Scotch giant, a learned pig, a child with two heads, and a lady with "lint-white locks", were exhibited. I found the pig was not so very learned, while the giant was not by any means gigantic, but both were fat enough in all conscience, and that was some compensation, at all events. The two-headed child was confined in a big bottle of spirits, and we were told that it had lived for three months, and had been visited in its lifetime by her Majesty and Prince Albert. I am very doubtful of this, however, for the heads appear to be composed of gutta percha, while the round body looks remarkably like a bag of chamois leather. The "shild" with two "'eads and four hi's," as the exhibitor has it, *may* be the real article, nevertheless, but, like the ghost of Hamlet's father, it comes in a questionable shape. Leaving this exhibition, I made my way to another, where a couple of melancholy bears are to be seen swaying their heads right and left, and back again like pendulums. There were also a few monkeys of different sorts, and a couple of wild Kaffirs, so called, who howled, danced, and wound up their entertainment by tearing a live rat to pieces with their teeth. I was told previously that the wild men devoured a rat between them at every exhibition, but certainly they did nothing of the sort while I was looking on. The "entertainment", however, was disgusting enough as it was, and, therefore, the least said about it the better. After this I visited "Theatres of Variety", and pavilions of "Standard" and "National" nomenclature, where clog-dancing, comic singing, tumbling, wry faces, and sensation dramas full of

A Dancing Bear.

murders, and five or ten minutes in length, were the order of the day. I looked into the wild beast menageries, and saw the old familiar faces of the lions, the elephants, the monkeys, and the mottled serpents many feet in length. I visited caves of "magic and mystery" where single hats were made to hold almost the furnishing of a room, and where shillings were changed into sovereigns at the word of command.

Outside the shows may be seen wonderful pictures of battles and wild beasts, where the air and the very ocean are alive with bullets and bursting shells, while the woods are literally swarming with ravenous beasts, reptiles, and birds of prey; and there is Hengler's Circus, towering above the other booths like Saul among the people. There are the hobby-horses, with and without tails, whirling round in never-ending circles, with riders in every stage of joyous excitement and terrification. There are the rifle-shooting saloons, with ranges of six yards, or thereabouts; and there is the pop-gun practice, with ranges of as many inches from the muzzle of the weapon to the face of the target. And then we have the "Keek-Shows", and the height, weight, blowing and boxing machines, mounted with brass and glittering like gold. There are the "Cheap Johns", with their endless chatter, and their Brummagem wares, doing their very best to persuade a discerning public that their knives were made to cut and their razors to shave. Nor must we forget the sweetie stalls, the ice and cream mixtures, the bundles of rock-sugar, the balls, the Chester-cakes, the gingerbread, and the oceans of coloured liquid called lemonade and ginger beer. The space between the shows is crowded with all sorts of people in all sorts of dresses, and lots of little children are looking around them from elevated points of view, on their parents' shoulders, with wonder-stricken faces. The brass bands are tearing away at a variety of tunes; gongs and cymbals are sounding here and there, bells are ringing, hoarse and "heloquent" men are bawling tremendously, and the din is absolutely deafening. It is hot and stifling; and no wonder, for everybody is squeezing his neighbour, there is not a breath of air, and the sun is glaring in the heavens. I am perspiring copiously outside, and dry as dust within; so, in these circumstances, I take leave of the Fair, and the reader at the same time, and — that's all.

GLASGOW HERALD 16 July 1864.

———————— * ————————

THE KIBBLE ART PALACE AND CONSERVATORY

On the invitation of Mr. Kibble, a company of ladies and gentlemen to the number of about 1500, assembled last night within his "Crystal Art Palace and Conservatory", Botanic Gardens, for the purpose of obtaining a private view of this elegant structure prior to its public opening, which is expected to take place in the course of a few weeks. ... Advantage has been taken of its transference to Glasgow (*from Coulport*) to enlarge and improve it in several important respects, and generally to adapt it to its new situation and future uses, ... The Art Palace is erected at the east end of the Gardens, near the principal entrance. The foundations are of stone, the structure itself being of glass and iron, and the internal supports consisting of graceful iron pillars. Entering by the main door, which faces the west, we find ourselves in the small dome, which has an area of 60 feet, and a height of about 34 feet. In the centre is a pond 27 feet in circumference, rising from which is an ornamental stand, containing pyramidal rows of flowers and miniature fountains. . .

Running down the centre of the moss house are three small ponds, in one of which will be set a tree showing a combination of 50 different mosses, skilfully interwoven. The corresponding transept on the left of the small dome is being prepared for the reception of a collection of models of ancient ruins and famous buildings, such as the Parthenon, the Temple of Jupiter, the Colosseum of Rome, &c. . . . Passing through the corridor which leads from the small dome, and, noticing by the way the pictorial effect which is obtained by a series of advertising transparencies fitted up in the roof, we enter the main Dome, a magnificent circular expanse, flooded with light, and, by its harmonious arrangement of flowers and tree ferns and statuary, forming an interior of striking beauty. The large Dome is 471 feet in circumference, and is carried on 36 iron pillars, arranged in two circular rows. Following the general design observed elsewhere the centre of the Dome is occupied by a pond 185 feet in circumference, the uses of which are as novel as they are varied. Underneath the pond is a chamber 14 feet in diameter, where it is proposed to place an orchestra, whose music will form a melodious mystery to strangers in the forthcoming festivities. The chamber will be so constructed that the sounds of the instruments may be admitted or shut out of the Dome at will, and in this way it is expected that charming diminuendo and crescendo effects will be obtained from the invisible performers. When this artifice is not employed it is intended to place in the centre of the pond a fairy fountain, which will throw up forty jets of water to a height of 35 feet, while electric lights placed in the roof will be directed upon the rising and falling spray, tinting it with changing hues of gold and silver, and all the colours of the rainbow. If, however, the requirements of a large audience are superior to all other considerations, the mechanical arrangements are such that in an hour the water may be discharged from the pond, which being boarded over will give sitting accommodation for some 800 persons. The large Dome is floored with iron fretwork, supplied by Messrs. George Smith & Son, and raised on timber sleepers. Underneath are about three miles of copper tubing, three inches in diameter, for the purpose of supplying heated air to the building. The Conservatory is abundantly supplied with gas, some 600 jets being ready for use after dark in the large Dome. The corridor connecting the two Domes gives entrance to a retiring and a refreshment room. All through the building are statues and busts of poets, composers, orators, and philosophers. The Art Palace has been erected under the personal superintendence of Mr. Kibble, by whose fine taste and large experience in the culture and arrangement of flowers, &c., it has greatly benefited.

GLASGOW HERALD 7 *May 1873*.

PRINCE OF WALES THEATRE.

Lessee and Manager...............................Mr. SIDNEY.

ON SATURDAY, DECEMBER 13,

Production of Mr. SIDNEY'S
FIFTH GLASGOW PANTOMIME,
Entitled
THE FAIR ONE WITH
THE GOLDEN LOCKS,

Rewritten and Arranged Expressly for this Theatre.

THE BALLETS by Mademoiselle De Rosa and her Troupe of
Charming Coryphees.
THE HARLEQUINADE by Messrs McNatty, Fulford, Fred.
James, Mademoiselle Amy, and Miss Tessie Herbert.
THE MUSIC Composed, Selected, and Arranged by
Mr. F. W. Allwood.
THE PROPERTIES by Mr. Lockheart and Assistants.
THE MACHINERY by Mr. Moffatt and Assistants.
The Beautiful DRESSES from Designs by Faustin
and D'Albert.
THE SCENERY by Mr. Swift and Mr. Dangerfield, and

TWO SPECIAL SCENES

The Boudoir of the Fair One, and the Giant's Glen — by Mr.
William Glover, to whom Mr. Sidney begs to tender his
public thanks for the great assistance rendered to this
production by Mr. Glover's masterly execution of the above.
The whole produced under the Personal Direction
of Mr. Sidney.

SPECIAL ENGAGEMENTS

Miss ALICE DODD,	Mdlle DE ROSA,
Miss LOUISE CRECY,	Miss NELLY MILTON,
Miss MINNIE GOURLAY,	THE SISTERS ARNOTT,

Messrs. McNATTY, FULFORD, FRED. JAMES,
and
MR. FRED. W. SIDNEY.
ALSO, THE
MARVELLOUS MAJILTONS —
FRANK, MARIE, AND CHARLES.

THE BAILIE *10 December 1879.*

Mr. Sidney's fifth pantomime was launched in presence of a bumper audience on Saturday, when "The Fair One with the Golden Locks" made her *debut* amid no little enthusiasm. For a "first night" the whole of the stage business and scenic arrangement went with wonderful smoothness and exactness. Owing, however, to the clamour kicked up by the "gods" throughout the evening, those of us in the lower regions could gain but a hazy idea of the plot, and of the quality of the libretto generally. I may say at once that the scenery is exceptionally effective. Nothing finer has ever been seen at the Prince of Wales. Specially noteworthy are the Tangled Brake, the Bank of the River, Fairy Land, the Transformation, and Mr. Glover's two scenes, the Boudoir of the Fair One, and the Giant's Glen by Moonlight. In response to several loud calls for the "penter", the several artists had to come to the footlights and acknowledge a series of ovations.

In the matter of spectacular displays, groupings, appointments, ballet business, and stage paraphernalia generally, Mr. Sidney is specially strong. The human form divine — female of course — is shown to advantage. Legs and "animated busts" there are in rich profusion. The ballet corps are quite too awfully handsome, and trips it in fascinating style. The weak point in the pantomime, I

Characters from a traditional Glasgow pantomime of 1883.

fancy, is "the words". This seems colourless, wanting in pith and point, and shows a plentiful lack of wit throughout. . . .
THE BAILIE *17 December 1879.*

———————— * ————————

Mr. Fred. Sidney does the major part of the fighting at the Prince of Wales. He is seldom off the stage, and his *lachrymoso* is one of the most amusing "bits" of broad comedy imaginable. But, indeed, "The Fair One with the Golden Locks" is altogether a marvel of mirth and fun.
THE BAILIE *24 December 1879.*

———————— * ————————

A NEW RESTAURANT

The restaurants of Glasgow are many; but originality of decoration is in inverse ratio to their numbers. Most of them make the supply of food their only mission in life; outward surroundings are nothing; and as long as the diner can wrestle with his chop on a fairly clean table-cloth, under electric light, they consider that mission adequately fulfilled. London, however, knows how to unite the skill of the cuisine with the art of the decorator, and it is after the style of a celebrated Metropolitan house that Messrs. McKillop have arranged the Grosvenor Restaurant, over which a party of pressmen were shown on Saturday. The new building is undoubtedly the finest in Scotland; if not out of London. The restaurant occupies two flats opposite the Central Railway Station, Gordon Street. The ground floor is occupied by the bar on the left hand, and the grill and luncheon rooms and oyster bar on the right, and in the back of the buildings are dining and tea rooms. On the upper flat — approached by a magnificent single flight of Pavonezza marble stairs — are smoke room, billiard room, dining and tea rooms, and throughout the building are numerous private rooms. The decorations are handsome and tasteful; magnificent without being gaudy. The staircase, hall, and corridor on the ground floor are decorated by means of glazed faience, specially designed and modelled. In style the ornament may be described as of free Renaissance character. . . . The general colouring of the work is a scheme of pale yellow and blue. An attractive feature of the upper floor design is the set of hand-painted tile panels that fill some of the spaces in the arcading. The panels are mostly architectural in subject and include some well-known edifices in Edinburgh, Glasgow, and London. . . .
EVENING TIMES *20 November 1899.*

CALAMITIES

Glasgow, as a great industrial city, has had its fair share of disasters, and a selection of these is included here. Many of them were unspectacular and affected only a small number of people, but I think it is important to remember that the loss of someone's nearest and dearest is a personal tragedy for them. One of the most astonishing facts to emerge is the number of disused coal pits where the shaft was just left open and unguarded, a perpetual danger to everyone around. The North Woodside pit is the most notorious and best documented of these places, although the Fullarton Pit at Tollcross comes a close second. Pit accidents were rarely in the form of explosions, but almost always the result of some mechanical fault, or simply carelessness. Theatre disasters are also common, both fires and panics, one example of each being included. Despite the city's importance as a centre of the shipbuilding industry, comparatively few disasters have taken place. By far the worst was the capsizing of the *Daphne* at its launching in 1883, with fearful loss of life. The collapse of Templeton's carpet factory six years later, is not so often remembered today, probably because the well-known Venetian landmark was rebuilt according to the original designs immediately afterwards.

----------------- * -----------------

LIEUTENANT SPEARING'S ORDEAL

On Wednesday, September 13, 1769, between three and four o'clock in the afternoon, I went into a little wood called North Woodside (situated between two and three miles to the north-west of Glasgow), with a design to gather a few hazel-nuts. I think that I could not have been in the wood more than a quarter of an hour, nor have gathered more than ten nuts, before I unfortunately fell into an old coal-pit, exactly 17 yards deep, which had been made through a solid rock. I was some time insensible. Upon recovering my recollection, I found myself sitting nearly as a tailor does at his work, the blood flowing pretty fast from my mouth; and I thought that I had broken a bloodvessel, and had not long to live; but, to my great comfort, I soon discovered that the blood proceeded from a wound in my tongue, which I supposed I had bitten in my fall. Looking at my watch (it was ten minutes past four) and getting up, I surveyed my limbs, and to my inexpressible joy found that not one was broken. I was soon reconciled to my situation, having from childhood thought that something very extraordinary was to happen to me in the course of my life, and I had not the least doubt of being relieved in the morning; for the wood being but small, and situated near a populous city, it is much frequented, especially in the nutting season, and there are several footpaths through it. Night now approached, when it began to rain, not in gentle showers, but in torrents of water, such as is generally experienced at the autumnal equinox. The pit I had fallen into was about five feet in diameter, but not having been worked for several years, the subterranean passages were choked up, so that I was exposed to the rain, which continued with very small intermissions till the day of my release; and, indeed, in a very short time I was wet through. In this comfortless condition I endeavoured to take some repose. A forked stick that I found in the pit, and which I placed diagonally to the side of it, served alternately to support my head as a pillow, or my body occasionally, which was much bruised; but the whole time I remained here I do not think that I ever slept one hour altogether. Having passed a very disagreeable and tedious night, I was somewhat cheered with the appearance of daylight and the melody of a robin-redbreast that had perched directly over the mouth of the pit; and this pretty little warbler continued to visit my quarters every morning during my confinement. . . . At the distance of about a hundred yards in a direct line from the pit there was a water-mill. The miller's house was nearer to me, and the road to the mill was still nearer. I could frequently hear the horses going this road to and from the mill, frequently I heard human voices; and I could distinctly hear the ducks and hens about the mill. I made the best use of my voice on every occasion, but it was to no manner of purpose; for the wind, which was constantly high, blew in a line from the mill to the pit, which easily accounts for what I heard; and at the same time my voice was carried the contrary way. I cannot say I suffered much from hunger. After two or three days that appetite ceased; but my thirst was intolerable; and though it almost constantly rained, yet I could not, till the third or fourth day, preserve a drop of it, as the earth at the bottom of the pit sucked it up as fast as it ran down. In this distress I sucked my clothes, but from them I could extract but little moisture. The shock I received in the fall, together with the dislocation of one of my ribs, kept me, I imagine, in a continual fever. I cannot otherwise account for my suffering so much more from thirst than I did from hunger. At last I discovered the thigh bone of a bull (which I afterwards heard had fallen into the pit about eighteen years before me) almost covered with the earth. I dug it up, and the large end of it left a cavity that I suppose might contain a quart. This the water gradually drained into, but so very slowly that it was a considerable time before I could dip a nut shell full at a time, which I emptied into the palm of my hand, and so drank it. The water now began to increase very fast, so that I was very glad to enlarge my reservoir, insomuch that on the fourth and fifth day, I had a sufficient supply, and this water was certainly the preservation of my life. At the bottom of the pit there were great quantities of reptiles, such as frogs, toads, large black snails or slugs, etc. These noxious creatures would frequently crawl about me, and often got into my reservoir; nevertheless, I thought it the sweetest water I had ever tasted. . . .

Saturday the 16th, there fell but little rain, and I had the satisfaction to hear the voices of some boys in the wood. Immediately I called out with all my might, but it was all in vain, though I afterwards learned that they actually heard me; but being prepossessed with an idle story of a wild man being in the wood, they ran away affrighted.

(*Lieutenant Spearing was not rescued until September 20th. Unfortunately his sufferings did not end then, for some time afterwards he had to suffer the additional misery of having his left leg amputated*).

GLASGOW PAST AND PRESENT *vol. II page 79.*

A SECOND ACCIDENT IN THE SAME PIT

It is rather remarkable, notwithstanding of the accident which had happened to Lieutenant Spearing in this coal-pit, that it had not been subsequently fenced round and secured from danger, in consequence of which neglect a similar misfortune as that of Mr. Spearing befell a woman in the same pit a few years afterwards, under circumstances extremely similar to those before mentioned; but she fortunately was relieved at the end of three days while Lieutenant Spearing remained there for a week. This female was a washerwoman, who lived in the neighbourhood of Woodside, her Christian name . . . was Janet, but her surname, I believe, is now unknown. She had received a quantity of linens and body habiliments from a Lady in Glasgow, to be washed, and to have the benefit of a few days' exposure to the sun upon the green fields of the country. These being ready and made up into a goodly load, she returned to Glasgow with them on her back. The lady being well pleased with the washing and the white appearance of the linens, not only paid Janet her full demand for her labour, but also treated her to a dram, and a *whang* from a kebbock, or skim-milk cheese, which she enclosed between two thick pieces of oatmeal cake or bannock, the same being the best part of a whole *farle*. This turned out a lucky circumstance for Janet who, with many thanks, after having secured her well-earned penny in her capacious leathern pouch hanging by her side, deposited the kebbock and the bannock in her apron, which she tucked up like a bag, and secured it behind her with a substantial brass pin. Thus equipped, Janet set out on her journey home. It was in the month of September or October 1773, and in the height of the nutting and brambleberry gathering season, and upon a Saturday evening, that the accident in question occurred.

The road to Janet's dwelling skirted the wood referred to by Mr. Spearing, and Janet on her way home had plucked a few ripe brambleberries from the bushes . . . when she observed some hazel shrubs in the wood with clusters of ripe nuts on them. She had obtained only a very few of these nuts when a beautiful cluster of rich filberts hanging on a shrub in a thicket caught her attention. . . . Janet . . . stepped rashly forward, and seized it; but, alas! at this moment, while firmly grasping this forbidden fruit, she fell headlong into the very same coal-pit so accurately above described by Lieuteńant Spearing. Janet was quite stunned by the fall, and for some time remained insensible; but, on recovering her recollection, she found herself lying at the bottom of the pit, with the fatal cluster of filberts still firmly grasped in her hand. Notwithstanding of the pit being about fifty feet deep, she had received no serious injury by her fall, and accordingly having gathered herself up, and given her clothes a little shaking, to put them to rights again, she began to examine consequences; but, unlike Lieutenant Spearing, who, on first recovering from the shock of his fall, immediately began to examine if all his limbs were safe and sound, Janet, with more Scotch prudence, began, in the first place, to examine her leather pouch, to see that none of her money had fallen out of it in the course of her descent, and to her great comfort she found it all safe and snug, not a halfpenny of it having gone amissing. She then commenced calling loudly for assistance, in the hope that some passers-by might hear her cries; but her efforts were all in vain, for no one approached her dreary abode, or heard the often-repeated and lamentable sound of her voice. At length, wearied and fatigued . . . she beheld darkness approach, and then she despaired of receiving any deliverance for that night; so she calmly unfolded her apron, and took a portion of the kebbock and bannock to her supper, and then quietly composed herself to sleep . . .

The next day was a Sunday, and Janet fondly hoped that some graceless weaver, or some blackguard collier, would be ransacking the wood for nuts, and would hear her cries; but in this she was again mistaken, for on that day she did not hear the tread of a single foot, or the voice of man; but ever and anon she distinctly heard the distant bells of Glasgow ringing their solemn tolls before church service began. ... Monday passed over like Sunday without a footstep being heard in the vicinity of the pit, so that poor Janet began to entertain the worst fears of her forlorn situation. On Tuesday, however, a labouring man happened to be passing, and fortunately heard the cries of Janet. On reaching the pit, he called down to her, inquiring at her if any accident had happened, when Janet informed him how she had fallen into the pit, and begged him to procure assistance for her relief; this was immediately got, and Janet again brought into the bright light of day, not a whit the worse of her three nights' immurement.

Not long after her deliverance, a match was struck up between Janet and her rescuer, and it would be well if the story, like most novels, had ended in a happy marriage; but, unfortunately, Janet's husband turned out an idle drunken fellow, who lived upon his wife's industry. Poor Janet, when excited by his miserable drunken habits, has been known, in bitterness of heart, to have exclaimed to him, that the Devil himself had certainly had a hand in bringing them together at the mouth of the Woodside coal-pit.

GLASGOW PAST AND PRESENT *vol. II page 84.*

---

*

On the evening of the 6th. instant, Thomas Urie, a collier at Strathbungo, near this city, fell into a waste coal pit and was killed. His brother had, that night, been on a visit to him and had convoyed him partly home, but, on his return to his house, having taken a bye-road to be nearer, he missed his way and unfortunately fell into the pit. His neighbours, in vain, searched for him the whole night, and, when found in the morning, he was dead, both of his legs were broken.

GLASGOW COURIER *15 November 1800.*

---

*

(On Saturday) Same day, when a labourer was working at the mouth of a coal pit a little south from Gorbals toll-bar, his clothes got entangled with one of the coal buckets, by which he fell to the bottom of the pit, and was killed on the spot.

GLASGOW HERALD *17 October 1806.*

Accident in a Coal Mine. — Thursday evening, between 6 and 7 o'clock, an explosion took place in a pit of the Dalmarnock colliery. The flames and dust ascended nearly to the top of the shaft; and fears were at first entertained that the whole of the workmen, consisting of about 40 men and boys, that were busily employed below at the time, had been killed. The explosion took place at the bottom of the shaft, which communicated with two seams of coal; and was ascertained to have been occasioned in consequence of a quantity of gas from the under seam escaping through the wooden scaffolding over the lower seam at the bottom of the shaft, which had ignited, and besides displacing about 18 fathoms of the partition, occasioned the death of a boy, who fell from a height of 13 fathoms to the bottom of the lower seam, and also severely burned 4 men and 2 boys that were working near the bottom of the shaft. The unfortunate individuals were instantly taken out and conveyed to their residences, and since that time have been constantly attended by a surgeon. Two of the men have been slightly injured, but the others have been burned very severely, and the life of one of the boys is considered very doubtful. The proprietor of the pit was engaged the most of the night in directing the workmen, and making every exertion in searching for the body of the boy missing; and, after having taken precautious measures, succeeded in finding it on Friday afternoon, between two and three o'clock, at the bottom of the under seam. The appearance of the body indicated instant death, and was severely mutilated by the fall. Fortunately the remainder of the workmen that were in the pit at the time escaped unhurt.

GLASGOW HERALD 6 *April 1829.*

———————— * ————————

THE DESTRUCTION OF THE THEATRE ROYAL, QUEEN STREET

It was a dull wintry day, the 10th of January 1829. Comparatively few passengers were to be seen in Queen Street or its vicinity; and their breakfast hour being past, the workmen had returned to the business of dismantling what had been the Royal Bank, preparatory to its conversion into the front part of the present Exchange, when the attention of a few individuals was suddenly attracted to what seemed a light misty vapour ascending from the lofty roof of the Theatre Royal. By rapid degrees this assumed the unmistakeable appearance of smoke — becoming each successive minute more dense and black, until first one lurid jet of fire, and then another flickered amid the darkness, to be almost instantly succeeded by one general outburst of flame. It soon became pretty evident indeed, that this Temple of the "Twin Muses" was threatened by the most serious of all theatrical calamities; and with winged speed did the intelligence spread over the city, as the fire-engines were dragged along in rapid succession to the spot — each attended by its crowd of followers, hastening with breathless speed to swell the general mass, assembled at every point from which a view of the burning edifice could be obtained —

> " — the mighty roast, the mighty stew to see,
>   As if the whole were but to them, A Brentford jubilee."

The Fire Brigade put forth, of course, on this occasion its mightiest strength; the measured strokes of the engine-men were heard without cessation; the water carts were hurried from place to place, with even a more than usual disregard of life and limb; the snake-like hose hissed in fifty different quarters, as they twisted along the streets, and scarlet-collared policemen looked on in unprecedented numbers — but, alas! the devouring element, as the newspapers have it, had resolved upon enjoying a satisfactory feast, and was not to be thwarted by the mightiest resistance that could be offered, so that in the course of a few hours this spacious structure was (*destroyed*).

VIEWS AND NOTICES OF GLASGOW IN FORMER TIMES
Stuart. 1848. page 110.

---

*

PANIC IN THE STAR MUSIC HALL

An appalling accident occurred on Saturday night in the new Theatre of Varieties, Watson Street, which resulted in the loss of 14 lives and the serious injury of a large number of persons. The cause of the disaster was one of those groundless panics with regard to which so much apprehension has been entertained since the similar catastrophe took place at the Sutherland Theatre. In course of the performance a cry of fire was raised, which carried consternation throughout an audience numbering fully 2000 persons. A rush was made to the several entrances. The occupants of the gallery and the pit met on the pit landing. A block in consequence occurred, and the lamentable loss of life took place in the fierce struggle which ensued for escape from the building. . . .

NARRATIVE OF RESCUERS . . .

Henry Holland, 13, Marshall Street: — I was in the Star Music Hall on Saturday night. I was seated in the balcony, over the gallery entrance. I went out on a pass with a lad named George Glasgow immediately before the trapeze performance. A number of people went out at the same time. As I was entering the gallery on my return I saw a man leap over the barricade at the end of the upper gallery on seats into the passage leading out of the gallery. He shouted "Fire, fire, fire," and said he was a detective. A panic at once arose. A number of lads dropped over the barricades and rushed down the gallery stair, and the whole audience seemed to follow. I went down with the rush. When I got to the bottom of the stair at the pit entrance, I saw an old man lying across the bottom of the stair. The people were falling over him. I did not fall, but on getting to the gate at the top of the staircase leading to the lane, I found it partly closed. A boy, who wore clogs, was jammed behind it, between the gate and the wall. George Glasgow, who was with me, helped me over the gate. I pulled out the lad who was jammed behind the gate. His face was black and blue, and he was quite dead. I also pulled out another young man. He did not seem much hurt. Somebody helped him downstairs, and I don't know what became of him. When I pulled out the two young men the gate swung open. When I went upstairs the gate was standing back to the wall. I don't know how it had swung round. I am quite certain the lad was jammed behind the gate. Inside immediately under the ticket-window, I saw a young woman lying. I think she was dead. There were several people lying above her, and the crowd from the gallery and the pit kept pressing forward. I took off my jacket and handed it through the window, and passed several persons through the ticket-window to a young woman and a gentleman in the box. The people lay in a great heap, and so packed together that I could not get them out from the side next the entrance. I passed inside and lifted them off the top. A policeman and a commissionaire were also engaged in passing the people through the window and in taking them into the pit.

GLASGOW HERALD 3 November 1884.

———————— * ————————

THE SHIP-LAUNCH DISASTER AT GLASGOW

The terrible disaster at the launch of a newly-built vessel on the Clyde, on Tuesday week, by which the lives of nearly a hundred and twenty working men were suddenly sacrificed, has occasioned great distress. It took place at Linthouse, Govan, below Glasgow, at the shipbuilding yard of Messrs. Alexander Stephen and Sons. The Daphne, a small steamer of 400 tons, built for the Glasgow and Londonderry Steam-Packet Company, was there launched into the water, just before twelve o'clock, having on board nearly two hundred men and boys who were to finish the internal fittings of the vessel. Somehow or other, the hull proved top-heavy on reaching the water, instantly turned over to the port side, and sank in the middle of the river. All the persons on deck were in a moment left struggling for their lives, and some escaped by swimming to the shore, or sought to cling to the upper side of the capsized vessel; some got hold of floating pieces of wood, or were picked up by the steam-tugs and a few boats that were near at hand. At high tide the hull was completely submerged, and the work of searching for the dead bodies, with grapnels from boats, was plied for some hours without much result. At low tide, . . . the vessel was seen lying on her port side, half the hull above the water, so that part of the deck hatchways could be opened and entered by the men engaged in this painful task. Eighty dead bodies have been recovered, some from below deck in the vessel, others from the bottom of the river. . . .

Messrs Stephen have launched 280 vessels, without any accident or loss of life. . . . Some of the dead are supposed to be still on board as there are many not yet found or accounted for. They are carpenters or joiners, riveters, engine-fitters, and plumbers, with their apprentices, caulkers, riggers, and labourers, many of whom have left wives and children, most of them belonging to Linthouse, Govan, or Partick. A subscription for the relief of the distressed families has been opened in Glasgow, and already amounts to between £8,000 and £9,000.

ILLUSTRATED LONDON NEWS *14 July 1883.*

---------------- * ----------------

THE COLLAPSE OF TEMPLETON'S CARPET FACTORY

The disaster in William Street, Greenhead, in the East End of the city, which occurred at a quarter past five o'clock last night, is much more serious than the late editions . . . indicated. It has now been ascertained that 51 persons have lost their lives by the sad calamity, and about 20 have received injuries. Altogether, something like 140 persons — all women and girls — were in the mill when the crash came, and only about half of that number escaped. The injured are being treated — some at the Royal Infirmary, and others at their own homes.

The building which succumbed was being erected to meet the demands of an already very extensive business, and although entirely independent, was meant as an addition to the old premises. The new factory, which measured about 200 feet long and 60 feet broad, and which was being built from plans by Mr. Leiper, architect, presented a very handsome appearance, and if it had been completed it would have been a prominent architectural feature in a district but scantily provided with imposing buildings. It was situated at the rear of the old factory, and fronted Binnie Place, the back or eastern gable towering above the one-story weft-weaving sheds attached to the present manufactory. . . . The manufacture to be carried on here was that of a new carpet fabric similar to what is known as the "Royal" Axminster, patent rights for which had been acquired by the Messrs Templeton from an American inventor.

The new building was still in the hands of the workmen of the contractor for the mason work, and was little more than a shell, although the roofing work would have been commenced in the course of a few weeks. . . . About a quarter past five o'clock, and shortly after the masons had left work, while a gale of extraordinary severity was blowing from the north-west, a gust of wind caught the wall of the new building which faces the west, and dashing it down, it fell with great violence against the eastern wall, with the result that the latter crashed with a sound like thunder through the roof of the weaving shed of the old mill. In this shed, which was about 200 feet long and 50 feet broad, there were 140 looms, at each of which a girl was engaged at work, under the charge of four male tenters. About 900 women and men were engaged in the mill altogether. No sooner had the crash of the fallen gable taken place than a general panic ensued, not only in the weaving shed, but in all the other departments of the building, as the whole mill, it is stated, shook as if an earthquake had occurred. Those who were uninjured by the falling of the mass of masonry into the weaving shed fled terror-stricken in the direction of the main door, which led to William Street. . . . Fully 70 of the girls escaped in this way, but many others who were uninjured remained by the side of their less fortunate companions, and bravely assisted them from the shed. . . .

Margaret McCulloch, who resides at 59, Waterloo Street, Calton, and who was buried in the ruins for an hour and a half before being rescued, says:— I was working near the wooden partition which divided the shed from the new mill. I worked up till five o'clock, but the usual stopping hour is six. As I had finished I intended to go home, but it occurred to me that I might clean up my loom, where I was busily engaged. The first thing I heard was a strange rumbling noise. I thought the boilers had burst. Then came the crash. I heard the bricks crashing through the roof, and suddenly all became dark.

I was struck on the head, but I do not know with what. My legs and arms were bruised. I was doubled up, my head being forced down to my knees. I was greatly terrified. I could not conceive what had happened, but I never lost my senses. I cried for assistance, and continued crying for a long time. My neighbour, Lizzie Finlayson, had been working at the loom beside me, and I would like to know whether she has escaped. I heard no sound or cry from her. After a while I heard the men working above me, and I kept on crying. By and by one of them put a stick through a hole and asked me to take hold of it, to see how far down I was. I grasped the stick. The men kept calling to me to "Cheer up, lassie; we'll be sure to get you out." That helped to keep up my heart. I was getting very weak and faint, but after a while the men got a hole made above me and handed me through a drink of water. That recovered me greatly, and in a little while I was got out.

Ex-Bailie Waddel, who was one of the first to be on the ground after the disaster, made the following statement last night:— I was sitting in my house in Monteith Row when the accident took place. The wind was very high at the time and was coming in fierce gusts. Suddenly I heard a sound like thunder, and ran out to see what had happened. On looking towards the mill I saw that the walls had collapsed. I made my way to the works. I found the courtyard filled with the workers, many of the poor girls in a hysterical condition. I made my way towards the weaving sheds. The whole place was in darkness, but a rescue party had been organised, and were relieving from among the *debris* such of the imprisoned workers as they found possible to reach. One of the workrooms had been set apart for receiving the injured, where they were attended by a number of medical men who had arrived. The fire brigade, and the salvage corps, who had been summoned, arrived simultaneously with myself, and lent every assistance in the work of rescue. Lamps and lanterns were at first used, but very quickly the electric light was introduced, and assisted materially in the work. As to the cause of the accident, my opinion is that the wind caught the heavy crane which stood on the top of the building, and that when the crane fell it carried the whole of the building along with it.

EVENING TIMES *2 November 1889.*

RELIGION

The further back one goes into history the more dictatorial a part religion plays. In the 17th century it assumed a particularly joyless and masochistic form, with blatant persecution as its chief weapon against non-conformity. In country places such unchristian behaviour continued far into the following century. However, in cities more enlightened ideas began to prevail, although a strong prejudice against Catholics and Episcopalians continued. Progressive ideas suffered a setback with the Secession of 1733 and the formation of a new and puritanical body, the meeting-houses of which were models of ugliness and discomfort. In general the Church of Scotland proceeded cautiously with innovations. One of the exceptions was the architecturally splendid St. Andrew's Church in Glasgow, erected over some twenty years as a symbol of the city's increasing prosperity. Its congregation, however, was refused permission by the Presbytery to use the organ which they had installed in 1807 to match its sumptuous interior.

The eccentric behaviour of the Rev. Neil Douglas affords some light relief in an age which took itself far too seriously. If anything, the Victorians were even more zealous over their religious duties and the 19th century was the great age of missionaries and evangelists. Perhaps the most successful of the latter were the Americans Moody and Sankey who came to Glasgow to convert the heathen, in 1874. They certainly sparked off a lot of enthusiasm which resulted in a lot of equally enthusiastic architecture.

*

SAINT ANDREW'S CHURCH

The magistrats represented that the council for a considerable time bygone had under consideration the building of another church, and that it was judged Bell's yeard would be a fit place, and that they the saids magistrats have had several meetings with Patrick Bell, merchant, for the purchase of his high yeard on the south of the Gallowgate burn, and in case a church should be built there it was necessary there should be an opening made from the Gallowgate street thereto. . . .

EXTRACTS FROM THE BURGH RECORDS *25 June 1734.*

David Cation, carver, gave in his account for carving corinthian leaves on 112 madellions on the intabulature of the inside of the church in Bells yeard now in building, carving 107 roses on do. intabulature, carving 200 foot length of mouldings on do., carving three composit collum capitals for the portico and masons squaring the same, carving an collum capital for do. and squaring the same and putting of the capitals around the south side and west end of the church and cornishes for the work, extending to £86 14s sterling, and by the said account he gives credite for £50 sterling . . . and that there remains of ballance £36 14s sterling; which account being laid before the dean of gild and annual committee to be considered, and being now considered by the council, they find the article stated for the three composit collum capitals too much and therefor restrict the ballance foresaid of £36 14s sterling of his account to £32 14s sterling, and ordain Arthur Robertson, late treasurer, to pay to the said David Cation the said £32 14s sterling.

EXTRACTS FROM THE BURGH RECORDS 8 *December 1748.*

————————— * —————————

AN EAST CAMPBELL STREET MEETING HOUSE

There was no restriction as to building churches or meeting houses on this property; and accordingly no less than three were erected in Campbell Street alone, all belonging to rival sects. On one side of the street was the meeting house of "The Old Light"; on the opposite that of "The New Light", which grinned across at each other in all the fervour of that puritanical exclusiveness and intolerance which so much characterised these bodies in the olden time.

I well remember the queer interior of these old meeting houses more than forty years ago, so very different from their present brushed-up aspect, with the then unpainted seats, clumsy candle-holders dangling from the roof; huge wooden pillars or props to the deep slanting gallery; funny-faced clocks, which ticked and struck unceasingly; the sour countenances of "the hearers"; and last, not least, the droll-looking beadles, one of whom had a wry neck, and used to *tack* from side to side of the long flagged passage, as he essayed to conduct the ungowned "preacher" from the still quainter session-house, with its sanded floor, fir chairs, and water stoup, up to the "poopit", and who, after his exertions, fell into a heavy, and by no means inaudible, slumber in the "bench" among the "auld wives" in red duffles and white mutches, who, from considerate regard to their auricular infirmities, were·privileged to occupy that conspicuous position, and gazed upwards at the preacher with outstretched necks, like a flock of startled cranes, or as the deaf mother of Saunders Mucklebackit in the *Antiquary*, when under inconvenient interrogation. Perched on the top of one of the pulpits was an artistic effort to convey the idea of Noah's dove, with outspread wings, and a branch in its bill. This remarkable ornithological specimen was painted yellow, rather corpulent, and at first sight might have been mistaken for a member of the duck family; but it improved on acquaintance, and did the artist great credit for perfect originality.

GLASGOW PAST AND PRESENT *vol. II page 484.*

———————— * ————————

TEN GUINEAS REWARD

WHEREAS, ANDERSTON RELIEF MEETING HOUSE WAS BROKE INTO on Friday night, or Saturday morning last, by some abandoned Miscreant or Miscreants, who have BROKEN the LARGE CHANDELIER, and TORN the PULPIT CLOTH — A REWARD of TEN GUINEAS is hereby offered to any person who shall give such information as may lead to the discovery and conviction of such offender or offenders.

GLASGOW HERALD *20 July 1807.*

———————— * ————————

SAINT ANDREW'S CHURCH
ORGAN FORBIDDEN

The Presbystery of Glasgow, at their meeting on Wednesday last, took into consideration the circumstance of an Organ having been used one Sunday about six weeks ago during divine service in one of the Churches of this city, and after deliberating at great length, a motion to the following purport was made and seconded, — That the Presbytery are of opinion, that the use of Organs in the public worship of God, is contrary to the law of the land, and to the law and constitution of our Established Church, and therefore prohibit it in all the Churches and Chapels within their bounds; and with respect to the conduct of the Clergyman in this matter, they are satisfied with his judicial declaration, that he would not again use the organ in the public worship of God, without the authority of the Church. . . .

GLASGOW HERALD 9 October 1807.

—————————— * ——————————

THE REV. NEIL DOUGLAS

There was, as we very well remember, a most extraordinary character of a preacher in this city, in the year 1817 . . . (He) starts up vividly before us, in his huge brown wig, and ancient habiliments, at a time when we were studying the law . . . in the University of Glasgow. Mr. Douglas, we may remark, was connected by marriage with some of the best families in Scotland. He had no church of his own, properly so called, but, with the money of his wife, he rented, for a moderate sum, the old original "Andersonian Institution", then No. 2 of Upper John Street. . . . The old, rev. gentleman, for he was now approaching his 70th year, had, somehow or other, imbibed, for reasons best known to himself, a tremendous amount of hatred against King George the Third, and "his prodigal son", as he called him, the then Prince Regent — afterwards George the Fourth. Nothing could soften his wrath, even in the pulpit on Sunday, against those Royal personages. Nor did they stand alone in that respect. He was equally fierce and furious against the then House of Commons for he did not hesitate, on diverse occasions, to declare from his pulpit, "that it was a den of the most infernal corruption"; and when he condescended at times to be somewhat more moderate in his language respecting *Parliament*, the moderation of it only consisted in this, that some of the members of the House, which he named, were bought and sold, like so many *bullocks*, in the market for filthy lucre, furnished by the devil! This was startling enough, and much stronger, a great deal, than any of the other most violent reformers of the day had ventured to utter; but still, as Mr. Douglas was a minister of the gospel, and otherwise highly connected, it was thought he was a sort of privileged person, entitled to say anything he pleased in his own "poopit". He soon found out his mistake, however, as we shall presently show. He had publicly announced a course of lectures to be given by him in the Andersonian on Sunday, on the "Prophecies of Daniel", &c. Amongst the first of these lectures, on a fine summer Sunday afternoon, to a crowded audience, he became perfectly furious in some of his *political* flights. He had the temerity to liken the good old amiable George the Third, then an invalid in Windsor Castle, as worse, in his mental and corporeal capacity, than Nebuchadnezzar, the king of the Jews; and, as for his son and heir, George, Prince Regent, he designated him as a poor infatuated creature, over head and ears in love with jolly Bacchus; and, as for his *concubines*, whose names and designations he also did not hesitate to give without a blush, he scattered them with awful blasts of fire and brimstone, without mercy. Crowds after crowds innumerable, ran to hear these absurd, or senseless "sensation lectures".

Nothing could withstand some of his vehement and ungovernable denunciations on these, to him, most kindred topics; yet, in many other respects, he was a most amiable, easy, and obliging man. He was in stature rather small; and in person, lean and lank, and sallow complexioned. But he had a voice terrible for its power; it might be heard a long way off indeed, from his pulpit, and those who once heard it could scarcely forget it again, it was so uncommon — scarce of the earth, earthy. When the perspiration came trickling down his lean cheeks, as it often did in summer weather in the course of his animated effusions, he would think nothing of throwing off his curly wig, and wiping his face with a large towel, always beside him in the pulpit — he never wore any gown — and when he resumed the thread of his discourse, after this momentary relaxation, he looked like some sepulchral spirit conjured up by the painters of old.

He was, we remember, on one particular occasion, very much tormented with a swarm of flies, joined with some wasps, buzzing about his ears and other places of his person; he tried frequently to clear them away, with his hands thrown out in the most fantastical manner, while he was launching forth, with some tremendous philippics, against Lords Sidmouth and Castlereagh, to whom he also bore a mortal grudge, as was evident from the whole tenor of his discourses. The insects, however, were again re-appearing, and tormenting him more than ever. It was an excessively hot afternoon, both outside and inside of the tabernacle. He stopped abruptly for a moment, and thrusting out his clenched fists, as if to catch a handful of them, and slay the insects, his tormentors, on the spot; — or suiting the action to the words, or the words to the action . . . he broke out with his exclamation, much to the astonishment of his numerous auditory — "Yes, my brethren, the *enemies* of our country will go to ——, as sure as I catch these troublesome and tormenting wasps"; but, opening his fists to gaze at his supposed capture, the vermin escaped and flew away, and he made this excuse to his auditory — "*Feggs*, my brethren, I've missed them." He then, after the half-suppressed titter of his auditory, resumed his awful battery against some of the conspicuous living statesmen of the day. . . .

... We have had the privilege of hearing, or listening, to very many preachers, of one kind or another, for more than half a century, but, of all the preachers we ever heard, none could excel the Rev. Neil Douglas, for stamping or thumping, or the hot fire of his eloquence, when he became fairly excited with his inflammable matter. Even the elder Kean, whom we have often seen on the boards of the old Theatre Royal, in Queen Street, in his Richard the Third, Sir Giles Overreach, and other characters, could not match, for vehemence of speech and rapidity of action, this old, celebrated Glasgow preacher. And if his "place of worship" — if that be a proper name for it — could have held 10,000 persons, in place of 500, we are persuaded it would not have contained all the numbers rushing and panting to hear him, on some of his grand occasions.

At last the Magistrates of the city got rather uneasy, if not alarmed, at the tenor of some of his extraordinary discourses which had reached their official ears. They, therefore, engaged three of the most expert town-officers of the city ... to go and attend the remainder of these lectures, and to be sure and take down, in careful memorandum, all he said, in particular about Nebuchadnezzar and the King, and the Prince Regent, and the House of Commons. ... Unfortunately for the town-officers, in their excess of zeal to get as near as possible to the pulpit, in order to catch the true sound of his voice, or the real *ipsissime verba* of his lecture, they squatted themselves down on the steps of the stairs leading directly to his pulpit. On his entrance thereunto, he soon eyed them, but he commenced the service with perfect serenity. This part of it decently over, he began to clear his throat for the real mettle. He soon looked down from one side of the pulpit, and then from the other side of it, fiercely eying the town-officers, clad partly in their red habiliments, and he began, literally, to give it them, perhaps not unlike one of the enraged bulls of Bashan, which we read of elsewhere. The congregation soon saw that there was something "brewing in the wind". On he came to Nebuchadnezzar, with some of his usual comparisons, stamping and thumping in the most tremendous style, far more violent now in his language than he had ever been before.

And then, how he did burst forth on the three town-officers themselves, whom he surveyed underneath him, scribbling away with their pencils and paper, and now looking at each other somewhat aghast, as much to say this is dread Sunday work certainly. He charged them as being a parcel of "infernal scamps, or spies, sent, *not* by Nebuchadnezzar, but by Beelzebub the Devil, from the Council Chambers, to entrap him"; and such was the vehemence of his personal wrath against them, and the dagger-like looks manifested by some of the congregation also towards them, that they became, at this stage, fairly *non-plussed*, and were glad to cease writing, and throw aside their pencils and their paper, and afterwards to strut with them away in their breeches' pockets; resolving to trust to their own unaided memories for the remainder of his lecture. . . . The like of it they certainly never heard, nor any person else in the city; so when they went to the Council Chambers, at the Jail, on the following morning, they told what had happened, as distinctly as they remembered, to the sitting Magistrates, which petrified their honours not a little in their own judgment-seat. . . . Within a very few days afterwards orders came from the Crown Counsel to seize — greatly to his own consternation — the person of the said Rev. Neil Douglas, as guilty of the crime of High Treason, or Sedition, and to imprison him in the Jail of Glasgow till liberated in due course of law.

He was INDICTED to appear before the High Court of Justiciary, at Edinburgh, on the 26th of May, 1817, on the modified charge of "Sedition", or of "wicked sedition", in his pulpit, as aforesaid. The three town-officers . . . were, of course to be the chief, or principal witnesses against the accused on his trial. In fact, on their united testimony, as contained in their written and subscribed precognition, . . . the Lord Advocate and his Solicitor-General and Advocates-Depute, confidently relied for a sure and speedy conviction against the reverend panel, who, by this time, had become much alarmed about it himself. In fact, everybody in Glasgow believed that he would be transported "beyond seas" to a certainty. But, as good luck would have it for him, at this important juncture of his fate, the town-officers began to dispute among themselves as to the real words, or the true meaning or import thereof, as they heard him on that memorable Sunday afternoon. The case, in short, against the reverend prisoner absolutely broke down, through the *lapsus* of their own chief witnesses. The Solicitor-General, Wedderburn, abandoned it, with some degree of mortification on his lips. The late unhappy, but now surprised and rejoicing prisoner . . . took the opportunity of stating in most respectful language to the Lord Justice-Clerk, ere he left the bar of the Justiciary Court, that he would never more lecture about Nebuchadnezzar, nor say any words derogatory of his gracious Majesty the King, or to the disparagement of both Houses of Parliament.

REMINISCENCES OF GLASGOW *Peter Mackenzie. vol. I page 446 et supra.*

The new Ramshorn Kirk stairs.

IMPROVING THE ARCHITECT'S PLANS

Even the venerable Ramshorn Church and steeple have been swept away, and this ancient fabric, of which the father of Professor Anderson was the first pastor, has been transmogrified by Dr. Cleland into a very uncouth-looking affair, with its ugly tower, and neck-breaking steps. After the plan of the present St. David's Church and tower had been given in to the Magistrates by the architect, Dr. Cleland took the said plans home with him *ad avizandum*, and he gave strict injunctions that no person whatever should have access to him for three days, so as to give him full leisure to improve the plan of the architect, and the result of these three days' labour was the present crypt and neck-breaking stair.

GLASGOW PAST AND PRESENT *vol. II page 129.*

ARGYLE FREE BEADLEDOM

To comprehend the whole plot of the Free Argyle drama would require a deeper insight into the mysteries of deaconship and beadledom than we have any hope to interpret; but, ... we may possibly convince some unbelievers that vestry convocations are not so dull and religiously solemn as popular opinion suggests, and we may further help to enlighten the stupid and sceptical regarding the profound feelings of charity which move certain Christian saints in these modern and degenerate days. ... We gather from the "Statement of Facts" put forward by John L. Graham (*the beadle*) that he has been subjected to a series of vexations which Job might have shrunk from, and which certainly the beadle has suffered with saintly patience and resignation. The afflictions which have pained him, it further appears, hold some mysterious connection with the office he has just quitted, since we learn that so far back as fifteen years ago the beadle's predecessor was harassed after a similar fashion. The beadleship of the Free Argyle may, in fact, be a permanent purgatory, bringing hereditary cares to any man bold enough to seek for the honour of this office. ... We learn that the first crime with which he is charged is the suspicious possession of half a crown. By a letter printed in evidence, it is shown that the half crown in question was bestowed as a "kind gift" by a member of the congregation on the beadle. ... A second charge laid against the

Enthusiastic singing in the Kirk.

unhappy beadle rests on his obtaining, under false pretences, a silver snuff-box, belonging to some unknown owner, but found somewhere within the sacred precincts of the Free Argyle. This definite charge again fades away into the fact that the beadle had picked up a twopenny tin snuff-box, belonging to his own child, containing a halfpenny and a few sweeties. This transmutation of tin into silver is an act of alchemy not unknown to "smashers" and the congenial fraternity they consort with. . . . But the unwary church official is blackened in the eyes of the Argyle congregation by charges of new and more daring rascalities. It is hinted that he broke into and plundered his own shop, and that under his eyes the Bibles of the congregation disappeared either by human or fiendish agency. Finally, not content with the charge of filching a silver instead of a tin snuff-box, the accusers of the persecuted man tax him with being a religious "smasher" who dispensed his charity to the poor in leaden shillings. This climax of villainy is really appalling, and . . . without grounds for making this heinous charge, we may ask what saint in modern times has suffered equal calumnies, and among the martyrs of our century the Glasgow beadle ought really to obtain a significant rank.

GLASGOW SENTINEL *19 May 1860.*

---------------- * ----------------

MESSRS MOODY AND SANKEY'S MEETINGS

Yesterday, a number of meetings were held, the principal one being in the evening, when all who desired to become Christians were invited to meet in the City Hall, the "overflow" being accommodated in the Greyfriars U.P. and St. John's Free Churches. The attendance at the City Hall was very great, and the crowding at the Albion Street entrance exceeded anything of a like nature we have seen for many a day. Men shouted and women screamed, and the excitement latterly rose considerably in consequence of several ladies fainting. The arrangements were not the best which could have been made, and for the sake of all parties it is to be hoped that some mode of admission which will obviate the unseemly disorder of yesterday afternoon will be adopted at succeeding meetings. The proceedings in the hall having been opened by praise, the audience engaged in silent prayer for a few minutes, in order, as it was stated, that the mind might be diverted from a consideration of the difficulties which had been experienced outside.

GLASGOW HERALD *2 March 1874.*

THOUGHTS ON THE SALVATION ARMY

I am not a soldier of the Salvation Army, yet I have no sympathy with those persons who can see in its pseudo-military organisation nothing save a burlesque, who can think of its rank and file only as vulgar brawlers, and who stigmatise its leaders as selfish and self-seeking hypocrites. Those who gibe and jeer at its military organisation are obviously lacking in sympathy with the militant spirit of our race, while to those who see only its noise and uproar, it may be answered that many respectable Ephesians must have considered St. Paul a very vulgar and pestilent fellow. As to the mode or method of Mr. Booth's life, and the curious interest manifested in his expenditure, it may suffice to say that even the Archbishop of Canterbury will admit that he who preaches the word shall live by the word, and sometimes in a palace with a princely revenue.

With this general defence of the Salvation Army, I will freely admit that the Army's proceedings are in many respects objectionable. The walls of Heaven are different from those of Jericho, and will not crumble away at the sound of those unmusical instruments with which Mr. Booth's followers unmake the Sunday quiet. A hysteric fit will not wipe out the evils of long years, the most brazen shouting will ascend on high no faster than the pious thought, and a man is not likely to be the better Christian because of a long record of unmitigated blackguardism. Sorrow and humility would better become some of the army's trophies than the exaltation which Dickens so cleverly satirised in his sketch of the converts to the Brick Lane Branch of the United Grand Junction Ebenezer Temperance Association.

The main point, however, is that the Salvation Army does reach and reclaim persons who could never be reached by the efforts of the Churches. It probably has reclaimed thousands of these persons. If it had only reclaimed a hundred, it might yet claim to have done great and good work.

QUIZ *28 March 1884.*

———————————— * ————————————

A CHILD'S MEMORIES OF CHURCH

My first attendance at church was made in (my grandmother's) charge. It was a U.P. church, and there was a plate in the vestibule, as was the fashion then in most Presbyterian churches. I am so old-fashioned in church matters that I still like to see a plate at the door, with elders standing on guard, and prefer, as it were, to pay before going in. The chink of coin, faint though it be, within the House, is to me an intrusion, a distraction.

On this occasion, however, the plate was very nearly my undoing. Misunderstanding my grandmother's gesture, and clean forgetting the penny in my glove, I was about to help myself liberally, when, deeply affronted, no doubt, she seized my hand and drew me indoors. Unwittingly I had saved my penny.

At that time the organ was beginning to be a burning question for the U.P. and Free Churches, and this church had not yet answered it. But there was a large choir, and, as our seats were near the front, I heard their voices well above those of the congregation; and above all the voices rose that of a bass singer, who fairly boomed. Thanks to him, I went home eventually, a sadly puzzled little boy. They sang "O God of Bethel", and the fourth line of it — "Hast all our fathers led" — came to my ears as "Has stole our father's lead". For quite a long time afterwards I associated the paraphrase with sundry great rolls of sheet-lead which lay against the wall at the corner of Bank Street, outside of the premises of Mr. Moses Speirs, the plumber, a person for whom I had the highest admiration and respect, and wondered if his father had lost much of the precious metal. . . .

To return to the church, the minister was a white-haired old gentleman with, I have been told, a most benevolent countenance; but he terrified me by repeatedly banging the Book, and from a word or two of his discourse I gathered that he was shouting about the Bad Place. I wanted to go home, till a glance at my grandmother informed me that she, at least, was not regarding the matter as urgent. She was, in fact, in the act of slipping an imperial — if you know what that is — into her mouth, and when she passed me another of the same, I was reassured. Afterwards I stood bravely on the seat while they sang, and all but ignominiously fell under it while they prayed. The penny in my glove, too, was really a great comfort. One could do so much with a penny then.

I REMEMBER J. J. Bell. page 85.

VILLAINY AND
THE LAW

The organisation of society presupposes a set of rules by which the community can regulate the activities of individuals for the benefit of all. Within the burghal system introduced into Scotland by the Normans, there were many rules or bye-laws introduced to protect the rights and privileges of the burghers. Penalties for those foolhardy enough to break the law, were harshly enforced — the idea of tempering justice with mercy is a modern concept. This chapter contains a selection of the bye-laws, some of the acts of villainy perpetrated over the ages, and some facts illustrating the punishment of offenders.

Human behaviour does not seem to have changed much with the passing of the years. Greed, violence, and drunkenness have always been with us, and as yet no effective deterrent has emerged to deal with them.

---- * ----

RULES FOR THE TOWN'S PIPERS

Iniunctiounes appoyntit to be gevin to Robert Spens and Fergus McClay, menstrales:

Item, that thai attend ilk mornyng and evenyng vpoun thair service diligently.

Item, that nane of thame have nather boy nor doig with thame quhair thai eit thair ordiner (*eat their dinner*).

Item, that thai stope na friemen that is hable to gif them ordiner, nor to tak syluer fra ane to pas to ane vther.

Item, that thai sall nocht misbehaiff thame selffs in na houssis quhair thai salhappin to eitt thair ordiner, bot to be content of sic as salbe presentit to thame be thame that thai eit with.

Item, that thai sall nocht enter in na cloissis, nayther mornyng nor evenyng, bot to pas throw the haill towne fra thai begyn quhill thai end, and to leiff af thair extraordiner drinking sua that thai may pas honestlie throw the towne in thair service, nor to leiff thair playing in ganging of the calsaye ather to masones or drinking, and to pas scharple throw the towne with ony cumyng to houssis.

Item, that ilk ane of thame sall ather mak calsaye or furneis men to mak calsaye be the space of xx dayes betuix and Witsoundaye nixtocum, and that thai sall mak vther particular work as thai salbe requirit.

And that thai keip thir iniunctiounes onder the paine of deprivatioun. Quhilk iniunctiounes the foirsaidis persones hes acceptit.

EXTRACTS FROM THE BURGH RECORDS 17 May 1600.

———————————— * ————————————

NO PIGS OR DUNGHILLS ON THE STREETS

James Inglis, baillie, being returnit from the conventioun of burrowis haldin at Selkrik, producit ane abbreuiat in wryt of the heidis of the said conventioun, togidder with ane copie if the Kingis Magesteis letter direct to Sir Jhone Drummond to be presentit to the conventioun of burrowis, in the quhilk speciallie wes contentit that na maner of fewall or fuilzie sould be had, laid, or keippit vpone the streitis, sein to ony persoun, or in ony pairt within bruche or citie, and that be rasoun the samein is nocht only vncumlie and incivill bot lykwayis verie dangerus in tyme of plaig and pestilence, and verie infective of itself, and siklyk that na maner of swyne be hadin within ony bruche or citie; quhairvpone the commissioneris of burrowis hes sett doun act and ordinance inhibiting and forbidding the same in all tyme cumming, and for taking away of the present fuilze hes appointit the space of xv dayis, vnder the pain of xl lib. to be vpliftit and tain aff the bruche quha pwttis nocht the said act and statute to executioun, as in the said statuit and act of burrowis at mair lenthe is contenit. . . .

EXTRACTS FROM THE BURGH RECORDS 16 July 1608.

———————————— * ————————————

CURFEW

The provest, balleis, and counsall, vnderstanding that certen insolent and prophain personis walkis in the nycht tyme vpone the calsie, abusing thame selfis and the nychtbouris of the toun, and gif the samen be nocht stayit great inconvenient may follow thairvpone heirefter, thairfoir it is defendit and forbiddin that na maner of persoun be fund walking vpone the calsie efter ten houris and efter the ringing of the ten hour bellis, vnder the pain of ten lib. and prissoning of thair personis at the discretioun of the magistratis, and this act to be proclamit; attour gif ony the said nychtwalkeris beis callengit be the magistratis or be the wache and makis recistance to be moir rigorouslie punischit be the sycht and discretioun of the saidis magistratis.

EXTRACTS FROM THE BURGH RECORDS *28 September 1608.*

————————— * —————————

KEEPER OF THE TOWN CLOCKS

George Smyth, rewler of the Tolbuith knok (*clock*), hes bund him to the town to rewll the said knok for all the dayis of his lyfetyme for the sowme of tuentie pundis money yeirlie . . . and siklike, oblissis him to rewll the Hie Kirk (*Cathedral*) knok and keip the same in gangand grath (*going order*), and visie hir twa seuerall dayis in the wik, the sessioun payand him ten merkis yeirlie.

EXTRACTS FROM THE BURGH RECORDS *27 January 1610.*

————————— * —————————

THIEVING

Dauid Jak, being apprehendit for thift, speciallie for steling of geis (*geese*) and vthir geir, and put in the stokis thairfoir be the constabillis of this burcht, and quha diuers tymes hes been challengit of befoir for the lyke, and banischit this burcht and baronie; siklyke, Donald McFeck, Hieland man, born in Kyntyre, being apprehendit for steling of plydis (*plaids*) and vthir small pykrie committit be him, ar baith ordanit to be scurgit fra the meilmercat to the brig end, and banischit this burcht and baronie foe evir; and gif evir they or ony of thame be fund or apprehendit within the same heireftir, of thair awin consent ar judgit and ordanit to be hangit; thaireftir the magistratis, dispensand with the scurging of the saidis twa personis, becaus of thair awin consent to be hangit gif evir they be apprehendit or fund within this burcht and baronie thairof hereftir, and presentlie to be put furth and banischit as said is this burcht and baronie.

EXTRACTS FROM THE BURGH RECORDS *23 November 1611.*

————————— * —————————

NOT PROVEN

Mathow Thomesoun, Hieland man, fidler, being apprehendit vpone suspicioun of forceing of ane young damesell, Jonet McQuhirrie, of aucht (*eight*) yeir ald, quhilk being denyit be him and hard to be verifeit, finding him ane idill vagabound, ordanis him to be laid in the stokis quhill the evening and thaireftir put out of the town at the West Port and banist the same for evir, and gif evir he be fund within this town heireftir, of his awin consent, to be hangit. . . .

EXTRACTS FROM THE BURGH RECORDS 25 *July 1612.*

----------------- * -----------------

THE UNEMPLOYED ARE NOT TOLERATED

It being fund that — Douglas was formerlie appoyntit to remove himselfe aff the toune, quhilk he hes not obayed as yit, and is brunt on the cheik and is knowne to be ane idle vagabound without ony laufull calling, he is therfor heirby ordained to remove aff the toune and all his, and that within ten dayes, and not to returne therto heirafter wnder the paine of scurging him throw the toune and benishing of this burgh.

EXTRACTS FROM THE BURGH RECORDS 24 *December 1660.*

----------------- * -----------------

UNPROVOKED ASSAULT AT LANGSIDE

The case of John Thomson and Agnes Walkinshaw his wife affords an additional example of the lawlessness and proneness to violence which characterised the latter period of the seventeenth century in the west of Scotland, . . . and helps us still further to form an idea of the manners and morals of the people. The case moreover shows, . . . that an unruly and lawless spirit did not pervade the lower classes only, but was participated in by persons in a better position in life.

In the year 1687, the tenants in the farm of Pathhead, near Langside, (*now the Queen's Park*) John Thomson and Agnes Walkinshaw his wife, without any cause or provocation, but probably from previous ill-will towards one of their neighbours, Mrs. Margaret Purdon, residing in the village of Langside, entered the dwelling "of ye sd Margaret", and having "shaken of all fear of God, dread or regard for ye laws, did invade and fall upon the person and bodie of ye sd Margaret, she being civilly sitting and spinding at ye wheel, and gave her many sharp and bload strokes on sevl pairts of her body, ding her to the ground, and puncing her with feet and hands, and oyr offensive weapons, soe that if it had not been the provedence of God and help of good neighbours, they had without all doubt have bereaved her of her good life."

For this unprovoked and most outrageous assault upon "ye sd Margaret", an unprotected female, she, with the concurrence of the Procurator Fiscal, raised a criminal libel against Thomson and his wife, who were called upon to appear before the Earl of Eglinton, the Sheriff-Principal of the County, and Principal Baillie of the Regalitie of Paisley, to answer thereto, on the 13th December 1687. They failed to appear, and offered no defence of their unlawful and merciless conduct, and therefore sentence was given against them in absence. They were fined in £100 Scots, and £10 of assythment or damages to the complainer, with the usual a alternative of imprisonment till payment. These sums were of very serious amount, and marked the Sheriff-Substitute's opinion of the character of the offence. . . .

SELECTIONS FROM THE JUDICIAL RECORDS OF RENFREWSHIRE
William Hector. 1876. vol. I page 46.

———————— * ————————

STATUTES AGAINST *Nestiness*

The magistrates and town councell, takeing to consideration the many complaints made be the inhabitants of this burgh of the growing and abounding nestines and filthiness of the place at present, doe therfore statute and ordain as followes, viz.,

Imprimis, that no master or mistres or heads of families or their children or servants or others lodgeing or resideing in their families shall, att any time heiraftir, be day or be night, cast out at their windows, aither upon fore or back streets or in lanes or closses, any excrement, dirt or urine, or other filth or water, foul or clean, under the pain of fyve merks Scots money for ilk transgression, and to ly in prison till they pay the samine and find sufficient caution to abstain frae such practises for the future.

Item, that none of the saids persons, att any time as said is, shall cast out, as is aforsaid, any excrement, dirt, urine or other filth, except water allenarly, at any jawholls, under the lyke penalty and hazard.

Item, that none of the saids persons shall, at any time as said is, cast out as aforsaid anything whatsoever out at these jawholls which have not a conduit to carry to the ground what shall be cast out therby, under the lyke penalty and hazard. . . .

Item, that no person whatsomever voyd or lay down their excrement of dirt or urine within any turnpyck or stair, or voyd or lay down excrement of dirt upon the high street, or other streets, lanes, closses, entries or passages within this burgh, under the pain of fyve merks *toties quoties*, and to ly in prisson untill they find caution as said is . . .

Item, recomends to the magistrates to putt these statutes, or any other former statutes and good customes of this burgh against nestiness and uncleaness, to full execution, and that they cause publication to be made heirof be tuck of drum that none pretend ignorance.

EXTRACTS FROM THE BURGH RECORDS *16 January 1696.*

---

*

COMPULSORY CHIMNEY SWEEPING

The magistrates and town councell, takeing to consideration the hazard, terror and amazement, as also the great prejudice that frequently falls out be soot takeing fire in chimney heads and braces, through the negligence and carlessness of the inhabitants in not sweeping of an keeping the same clean, therfor they statute and ordain that, in all tyme comeing, the haill inhabitants of this burgh shall, once every quarter of ane year, sweep and make clean the haill braces and lums possesst and keeped in constant use be them, whether they be of kitchines, halls, chambers, backhousses, brewhousses, smiddies or others whatsomever, and such other chimneys and braces that are not keeped in constant use to be sweeped at least once every year, and that under the pain of fourtie shillings Scots for each faillie; and in caise any fire shall break out in any brace or chimneyhead, through the defect of not tymeous sweeping therof as said is, the persons guilty shall be lyable to the fyne of ane hundreth pounds Scots, and punished farder in his person, att the will of the magistrats; and appoints the magistrates to make publication therof.

EXTRACTS FROM THE BURGH RECORDS *16 January 1696.*

---

*

HARSH PUNISHMENT FOR BEING RUDE TO THE PROVOST

The magistrates and town councell caused read in their presence a lybell raised at the instance of Charles Stewart, procurator fiscall, against Alexander Thomsone, baxter (*baker*) and burges of the burgh of Glasgow, for uthering many vyle and ignominious words against and insolent carriage and behaviour towards the provest, upon the said Alexander his being incarcerate within the tolbooth of the said burgh, for not giveing bond to make sufficient bread, conforme to the town councell their former act, dated the twentie seventh day of June last, as in the said lybell more specially and fullie is expressed; and Robert Rodgers, ane of the baillies, being presis in councell in the mater forsaid, the said Alexander Thomsone compeared and in presence of the magistrates and town councell he judicially confessed and acknowledged the haill words, expressions and insolent carriage forsaids, specially contained in the said lybell, and subscryved his said confession with his hand judicially as said is; which lybell and confession forsaid being considered by the saids magistrates and town councell they heirby amerciate and fyne the said Alexander Thomsone in the soume of fyve hundreth merks Scots money, to be payed to the said fiscall, and declares him to have no priveledge of a burges or gildbrother of this burgh in tyme comeing, and appoints the baillies or any ane of them to bring the said Alexander Thomsone to the head of the tolbooth stair (where publict proclamations uses to be made) upon Munday nixt, being the sixth instant, att eleven of the clock in the forenoon, and there to stand till twelve of the clock, with his head uncovered and a paper affixed on his brow containing the words following writtin theron, viz., *he stands here for vyle and ignominious words against the provest.* As also, appoints the saids baillies to cause his burges ticket (now given in be him in councell) to be torn and cancelled be tuck of drum, upon the place and att the tyme forsaid, and get bond and sufficient caution from him to leave this burgh and not to return therinto, and appoints him to ly in waird untill the said sentence be satisfied and fulfilled, and farder declares and ordains that if any person or persons baik or trade for him or with him, in tyme comeing, they shall be prosecute and punished as packers or peilers with unfreemen, and as to the said fyne allowes the magistrates to take bond therfore.

EXTRACTS FROM THE BURGH RECORDS *4 July 1696.*

---

*

Broke out of the JAIL of GLASGOW,
On Monday morning last, 9th curt.
HUGH SHEDDAN, aged about 18 years, a thick well-set, little black lad, was under sentence of transportation, for culpable homicide, whoever apprehends the said Sheddan, and conveys him to the said jail, shall receive Five Guineas rewrd.

GLASGOW MERCURY *19 March 1778.*

BYE-LAWS OF 1781

Whereas it is of great consequence that every regulation calculated to improve the police of the city should be adopted, and that at the same time every irregularity injurious to the inhabitants should be suppressed and prevented. The magistrates hereby give notice, recommend, and enjoin what follows, viz. —

That all proprietors of houses in this city shall, as soon as the season will admit, remove all water-barges, and fix and erect rones and pipes for the purpose of conveying the water from the eaves of their respective buildings, so constructed as to prevent loose slates from falling upon the streets; and it is recommended to those of the inhabitants who have already conveyed down their water in this manner that they will cause their pipes to be lengthened so as to prevent inconvenience to the public in rainy weather.

That all proprietors of houses or lands do give strict orders that the flags (*pavement*) opposite to their respective properties be regularly cleaned every morning, that so this valuable improvement may not be rendered useless to the inhabitants.

That all persons using ladders for repairing houses shall remove the same every evening before sunset, and no mason or slater, or any person working on the roofs of the houses in this city, shall throw over rubbish of any kind without keeping a person as a watch to prevent danger to the inhabitants.

That the person or persons having property in dunghills in the closes opposite to which the dung of the street is laid down, shall remove the same in twelve hours after it is collected by the scavengers, and no dung going to the country will be suffered to remain on the street after sunset on any pretence whatever.

That no person shall shake carpets, or throw water or nastiness over any of the windows of this city.

That no carter shall, on any pretence, presume to ride upon his cart, or to drive hard through the avenues or streets of this city. And as many accidents have happened through the carelessness of carters, particularly on the road leading from the canal, the magistrates hereby order and direct all carters to lead their horses short by the head, and it is earnestly recommended to the inhabitants to give information of the names of all who shall offend in this particular; that practices so dangerous to the public may be prevented, by punishing the guilty in an exemplary manner.

That all horses going to water shall on no pretence be rode hard, nor shall any person be permitted to gallop through the streets or avenues of this city.

That no persons having charge of buildings shall lay down stones upon the pavement at the side of the street allotted for the inhabitants, nor shall any person be permitted to slack lime upon any of the streets of this city.

That in all time coming, the practice of selling salmon by the hand shall be discontinued, and no person shall be permitted to sell in any other manner than by weight. . . .

GLASGOW MERCURY 22 March 1781
quoted in Glasgow Past and Present vol. III page 193.

———————— * ————————

PUBLIC WHIPPINGS

Yesterday, agreeable to a sentence of the Magistrates, Andrew Monach, for several acts of theft, was whipt by the hands of the hangman, through the principal streets of this city; although he is not above eighteen, he has been an offender for several years.

GLASGOW MERCURY 20 January 1785.

———————— * ————————

Yesterday, John Johnston, convicted of theft, was, agreeable to a sentence of the Magistrates, whipt by the hands of the hangman, through the principal streets of this city, and banished under the usual certification. Although apparently not above twenty years of age, the ignominy of the punishment seemed not to affect him. He was not above three hours out of prison, till he was recommitted for stealing some children's clothes, which were drying at the north end of the town.

A boy was committed to prison, for picking pockets in the crowd, while Johnston was whipping.

GLASGOW MERCURY 14 April 1785.

———————— * ————————

POACHING

WHEREAS, the grounds of
CASTLEMILK have, of late years been
infested with Poachers — This is to intimate
that a Reward of HALF-A-GUINEA is offered to
all the farmer's servants, and people in the
neighbourhood, who shall inform against any
person found shooting on the grounds of
Castlemilk, who have not a permission in writing
from Lady Stuart.

GLASGOW COURIER 23 September 1800.

EXECUTIONER

Wanted, for the City of Glasgow, an Executioner.
The bad character of the person who last held the
office having brought upon it a degree of discredit,
which it by no means deserves, the Magistrates are
determined to accept of none but a sober well-behaved
man. The emoluments are considerable.
Applications will be received by the Lord Provost,
or either of the Town Clerks.

GLASGOW PAST AND PRESENT *vol. I page 333.*

———————— * ————————

PRISON CONDITIONS IN 1804

Memorial for the lord provost and magistrates of Glasgow relative to
the state of the jail. In consequence of complaints . . . respecting the
state of the jail, the memorialists, on the 18th of May, visited and
minutely inspected it, and they are sorry to say they found the
complaints in several particulars well founded. The principal
grounds of complaint may be reduced to two; first, certain abuses

Saturday in the Police Office in 1825.

existing in the internal management of the jail and the treatment of the prisoners; secondly, the decayed state and the want of the furniture absolutely necessary for the accommodation of the prisoners. With regard to the abuses in the internal management of the jail . . . they consist chiefly in the want of due attention to the cleanliness of the jail, in the exaction of money from the prisoners in the name of dues, which are not sanctioned by any regulations relative to the jail, and in the scant supply of water afforded the prisoners.

With regard to the second ground of complaint, . . . the state of the bedsteads in the prison has long been a subject of complaint. From the decay and rottenness of the wood a great many of them are altogether useless, and a number of the prisoners are reduced to the necessity of sleeping on the floor. In the beginning of last year the bedsteads became so infested with bugs that for some time the prisoners could not use them. . . . The memorialists beg leave to suggest that in place of wooden bedsteads cast iron ones should be procured. The expence of cast iron bedsteads will no doubt be greater at first, but as they will very seldom require to be renewed, they will probably in the end be found cheaper than wooden ones. . . . The other articles of furniture, such as tables and chairs, are also much decayed, and require to be renewed. The presses, too, in several apartments, are infested by mice, which destroy the prisoners victuals, and some little repairs are necessary for excluding the vermin. . . .

EXTRACTS FROM THE BURGH RECORDS 8 *June 1804.*

ROBBERY & REWARD

LAST night, JAMES BROWN, merchant, was attacked by two men, between the Toll-Bar at the head of Gorbals, and the Fire Works, and robbed of his Pocket Book, containing upwards of One Hundred and Fifty Pounds in Cash and Bank Notes: besides some Accompts.

The Villains, when they made up to him, seized him by the arms, tied a napkin round his eyes and his hands behind his back, and threatened his life if he made any resistance.

A REWARD of TWENTY POUNDS Sterling will be given to any person who will give such information as may lead to a discovery of these two Men who appeared to be stout made and to have darkish coloured clothes.

GLASGOW COURIER *18 December 1804.*

GLASGOW HERALD *21 October 1805.*

———— * ————

BODY-SNATCHERS

Resurrectionists. — On Wednesday night, about eight o'clock, a fellow hired a noddy at the Cross, and told the coachman to drive to Little Govan. — On the way they halted to take in another person, whom the individual who engaged the vehicle described as his servant. — When the party had got about a quarter of a mile past the Gorbals Church Yard, the coachman was directed to drive up a by-road, where he observed three or four fellows with shovels over their shoulders, when the servant inside was ordered by his pretended master to go and fetch his luggage. — In a short time the luggage, a large well-filled sack, was brought, and thrown into the noddy, when the driver was ordered to push back again to town with all possible dispatch. — As no particular instructions had been given with regard to the place where the *gentlemen* wished to be set down, and as the driver had been ruminating in his own mind with regard to the characters of his customers, and the contents of the bag, he thought he could do no better than drive the party straight to the Police Office.

No sooner had he come to this conclusion than "smack went the whip — round went the wheels," and he ne'er halted until challenged by Captain Graham at the corner of Bell Street for furious driving. Coachee, however, who was now become big, and anxious with regard to the fate of his adventure, merely called out to the Captain to follow, if he pleased, as he had two gentlemen inside

Modern medical education — bodysnatching in the 1820s.

most anxious to see him on particular business at the office, and on he went pell-mell to Albion Street; but unfortunately one of the miscreants contrived to make his escape before the driver could possibly descend, and the other, who proved to be a fellow of the name of Bell, a well-known resurrectionist, and an associate in trade of Gillies and McLuckie, was seized by the collar when endeavouring to follow his companion. The contents of the sack proved to be the bodies of a male and female, one of which had, to all appearance, been in the grave for three or four weeks. — As the coachman had got no hire from the vagabonds, Bailie Gray, the Sitting Magistrate, ordered him to be paid from the Police funds for the good behaviour which he had displayed in the affair.

GLASGOW HERALD *11 September 1829.*

———————— * ————————

Church-Yard Thieves. — Friday morning, about four o'clock, as one of the watchmen in Calton was going his rounds, he observed a great-coat lying close to the gate of the burying-ground in Clyde (Abercromby) Street. Anxious to ascertain to whom it belonged, he stepped forward and demanded admittance; but the key, it was pretended by those on guard, could not be found. This had the effect of awakening his suspicions; and, determined if possible to prevent the violation of the grave, he clambered to the top of the dyke, when he observed a man squatted on the top of a grave. Not possessed of the firmest nerve, and being afraid he would be overpowered, the watchman called out for assistance, when the fellow started to his feet and was out of sight in a moment. The ground was thereafter examined, when it was found that the thieves had not been inactive — two graves having been robbed of their contents, and several feet of the third dug, and the head of the coffin smashed in. The bodies were both buried on Wednesday — the one was that of a soldier, and the other a female about 80 years of age. Two of the guard were, without much ceremony, apprehended; and in the course of the morning Serjeant Leckie succeeded in ferreting out and securing other three; one of whom, it appears, is the fellow who, a short while ago, was, by the dexterity of a noddy-driver, taken to the Police Office, instead of being driven to another quarter of the city. The party were despatched to the Sheriff's Chambers.

GLASGOW HERALD *15 March 1830.*

———————— * ————————

THEFT OF WASHING

FRANCIS WALKER and JOHN CONWAY, charged with stealing shirts from a washing-green near Govan, on the 26th February, were found Guilty, and sentenced to 14 years' transportation.

GLASGOW FREE PRESS *7 May 1834.*

———————— * ————————

A LUCKY ESCAPE

A "Giantess", who has been for some time past exhibiting herself in a booth at the foot of Saltmarket, was, on Monday, taken to the Police Office for examination, in reference to the sudden death of her husband. It was alleged that the parties had been drinking on Saturday night, when they quarrelled, and that the giantess struck her *smaller* half a blow on the head with a heavy piece of wood, which caused a deep wound. On Sunday, he died, and a rumour was raised that his death was caused by the injury, which led to the apprehension of the female. A surgical examination of the body, however, has taken place, from which it appears that no connection can be traced between the injury on the head and the cause of death. The giantess has accordingly been liberated.

GLASGOW HERALD *12 March 1841.*

———————— * ————————

ANOTHER VIEW OF THE FAIR

Thieving at the Shows. — Saturday night last appears to have been a productive one for the group of idle blackguards infesting the vicinity of Jail Square, and preying upon those who are foolish enough to congregate at this spot to gaze upon the tom foolery of the showmen. No fewer than six tradesmen were relieved of their watches on this occasion, not to speak of numerous petty thefts and attempts that occurred, and which, to save the parties trouble were never reported to the police. Truly, cautioning people against wasting their time at the shows, seems to have no effect; and so long as the authorities permit exhibitions to exist at this season, so long will crime continue to increase. It is a well-known fact, that yearly many youths of both sexes date their ruin from the Fair — police cases of every sort are augmented — police officers are overworked — and the persons who obtain most benefit are the mountebanks, thieves, and gamblers, who look forward anxiously to this annual gathering, from which they reap a rich harvest at the expense of the simple.

GLASGOW HERALD *2 July 1855.*

£200 REWARD

ABSCONDED from Glasgow, on Saturday, 22nd April, 1865, JOSEPH HUME WRIGHT, Warehouseman, Ingram Street, charged with extensive Frauds on a Foreign House, by substituting Coals in Cases consigned to them, and represented by him to contain Printed Muslins. Description:— 33 years of age; about 5 feet 8 inches in height; very thin sharp nose, and pretty prominent; very slight whiskers, and lightish hair, inclining to red, rather full on and under chin; very thin make in person. Generally dressed in frock coat, buttoned up; sometimes wore a darkish tweed dress. Had gold watch and chain; carried with him a large glazed leathern bag containing wearing apparel and under-clothing, and is believed to be possessed of a considerable sum of money.

The attention of the Police, Railway and Steamboat Officials, Shipping Agents, Hotel-keepers &c. &c., is specially called to this Notice. It is believed his intention was to take shipping for a foreign port. A Criminal Warrant has been issued.

The above Reward will be paid for such information as shall lead to the apprehension of Wright, by the Subscriber, who acts for the Agent of the Consignees.

HENRY MILLER
Trade Protection Society's Offices
Glasgow, 19th May, 1865.

GLASGOW HERALD *29 May 1865.*

FASHIONS

Fashions by their nature are ephemeral, and that is illustrated in this chapter by the inclusion of things other than clothes with which the word these days tends to be chiefly associated. Beginning with that ludicrous 18th-century code of honour which demanded satisfaction for every imagined slight, it continues with a selection from the mass of detailed information available on fashionable dress in the following century. In considering this subject, it is probably our sense of colour which has changed most. How drab our present-day clothes look in comparison with those of 150 years ago! On other matters we find such surprising things as a Georgian cigarette-lighter rubbing shoulders, as it were, with that old standby of coal-fire days, the briquette. Matrimonial fashions also appear in the form of two interesting but somewhat enigmatic quotations.

---

*

A MATTER OF HONOUR

On Tuesday last, in consequence of a misunderstanding between a Captain B — and a Mr. O — at the Theatre here, the preceding evening, the parties, accompanied by a Capt. McK — as second to the former, and a Capt. C — as second to the latter, met in a field in the neighbourhood of this city, and, after exchanging shots, the matter was settled to the satisfaction of both parties.

GLASGOW COURIER 23 April 1795.

---

*

FASHIONS FOR JANUARY

Full Dresses. — 1. A round dress of plain white muslin, made short in front, with a very long train; the body quite plain with a large tucker drawn round the bosom; the bottom of the dress bound with white ribbon, and trimmed with deep lace. The hair dressed in ringlets.

2. A dress of white muslin, with a drapery of the same, trimmed with gold or lace. The sleeves full and looped up with a diamond button. The hair ornamented with a bandeau of diamonds and ostrich feather.

November fashions in the Regency period.

Walking Dresses. — 1. A short round dress of white muslin, with a light blue Kerseymere pelice, laced up the front in military stile; a bonnet of blue to correspond with the dress ornamented with a military feather.

2. A Dress of white or coloured muslin, with a Spencer of black velvet. A black velvet bonnet. Silver bear Muff and Tippet. . . .

Observations. — The prevailing Colours are geranium, rose, blue and purple. The dresses continue to be made very low, and the sleeves quite plain with lace let in; lace tuckers drawn round the bosom. Pelices of all colours are universally worn; but black velvet or light blue Kerseymere are the most genteel.

GLASGOW COURIER *12 January 1804.*

——————— * ———————

EDINBURGH SHAWL WAREHOUSE
88, BUCHANAN STREET
FOR SHAWLS ONLY.

(Removing at May to No. 47, Buchanan Street, New Building, opposite the Arcade.)
DAVID KEMP respectfully informs his friends and the public in general that he is now daily receiving the *New Spring Pattern Shawls*, many of them quite novel in the style and very beautiful. He has also an excellent choice of *New Bordered Indiana Shawls*, now so universally admired for their beauty, comfort and

durability. As it frequently occurs that the Middles of Shawls wear out, while the Borders remain good, D.K. begs to state that he supplies *New Middles and Fringes* of every Fabric and Colour at a trifling expense. Particular attention paid to the *Cleaning and Refinishing of Shawls*. Charge for Cleaning and Refinishing *Silk Shawls*, 1s; *Thibet* and *Indiana Do.*, 1s 6d; *Real Indian Squares*, 2s; *India Long Shawls*, 3s; An excellent choice of every thing connected with the Shawl line.

Removing at May to No. 47, Buchanan Street, first Shop below Messrs. Finlay, Carvers and Gilders, exactly opposite the Arcade.

GLASGOW HERALD 7 March 1834.

---

*

EVENING AND OPERA COSTUME. — A robe of celestial blue satin, opening *en tablier*, over a white satin skirt, and trimmed down the fronts with white blond; five moss roses are placed along this edging, and from the three lower ones, little garlands of roses cross over the white satin. *Corsage a la pucelle*, blond lace *Sevigne*, with a rose on each shoulder, and in the centre of the bosom smaller ones reaching thence to the point of the waist; double sabot sleeves, a rose confining the fullness. *Coiffure en cheveux*, adorned with *agraffes* of gold and a beautiful spiral garland. Pearl necklace, gold ear-rings, with pearl drops.

PREVAILING COLOURS FOR APRIL. — Citron, jonquil, lilac, vert de Paradis, pale blue, and rose colour.

GLASGOW FREE PRESS 5 April 1834.

---

*

GENTLEMEN'S FASHIONS

WALKING DRESS. — A sky-blue frock, made double-breasted; the collar and breast to roll to the waist; the skirts and breast are faced with satin, the colour of the cloth, and the collar is velvet of corresponding colour. Waistcoat of brown figured velvet, single-breasted, with a close folding collar. Trousers of yellow drab elastic kerseymere.

DRESS COAT. — The most fashionable colour is the mulberry of all shades. The dress coat is cut rather longer in the waist, the backside seam more straight; the hip buttons not to spring, but to stand within from two inches and a quarter to two inches and a half apart; the skirts narrow, and the coat rather shorter; lappels rather shorter in front, and by no means to look downwards; the buttons at lappel to stand near the edge, and then gradually thrown back towards the eye. The collars are lower behind, and the whole breast is boldly thrown back, which shows to advantage the breast facing; this is always of satin the colour of the cloth. It must be remembered that the satin breast facing comes to the edge of the lappel facing, consequently, on the turn-over side there is no cloth seen but the stripe of cloth called the lappel facing. The collar is either of cloth or velvet, same colour. . . .
GLASGOW ARGUS 8 May 1834.

———————— * ————————

NOVELTIES IN SHAWLS MANTLES AND PALETOTS.

DAVID KEMP respectfully invites attention to his recent Extensive Purchases of FOREIGN SHAWLS, which have now come to hand, viz.:—
A Magnificent Choice of RICH WHITE, BLACK, and COLOURED PARIS LONG SHAWLS, Superb in Design, and Manufactured ENTIRELY OF WOOL.

Also, a Splendid Assortment of RICH LONG SHAWLS, with TWO, THREE, and FOUR FACES, enabling the Wearer to vary the Colour of Shawls at pleasure; these are most useful, and in Design, MAGNIFICENT and NOVEL.

PAISLEY SHAWLS and PLAIDS in immense Variety, and very Cheap.

TARTAN PLAIDS and SHAWLS of an ENTIRELY NEW STYLE and CHARACTER, manufactured by Mr. CROSS of GLASGOW, and especially admired and selected by the QUEEN at BALMORAL. These PLAIDS are, in many instances, made from the NATURAL or UNDYED WOOL, and are the most Chaste Style which has appeared this Season.

CLOAKS, MANTLES AND PALETOTS

In all the NEW STYLES, made in RICH GENOA VELVET, COLOURED and BLACK SATIN. MANTLES, with the NEW TRIMMING and a Splendid Variety of MANTLES and

PALETOTS in the NATURAL WOOL, and other Colours, decidedly the most Beautiful and Novel Cloak that has appeared. Prices commencing at ONE GUINEA.

47, BUCHANAN STREET.

GLASGOW HERALD 13 October 1848.

———————— * ————————

ORNITHOLOGICAL HATS

THE prevailing fancy for birds, small and large, light and dark, on the wing or at rest, on chapeaux of all kinds, is charming; but it does give one an oppression of the heart to think of the number of feathered songsters whose notes are hushed by this caprice of fashion. Why not let the birds live, and wear flowers? Velvet flowers and leaves are obtaining very well just now, and they really make a lovely rich-looking trimming for autumn hats and bonnets. Velvet is the trimming *par excellence* for autumn and winter millinery, also the material *par excellence* for autumn and winter dresses, and it is probably the most becoming of all fabrics near the face. It exerts a refining influence over the features, and apparently whitens and softens the skin. Droll as it sounds, alligator's skin is very much used as a trimming both for millinery and dressmaking purposes.

QUIZ 5 October 1883.

June fashions on parade in 1825.

THE UMBRELLA

NOW-A-DAYS the umbrella plays a most important part in our domestic economy. How different from some years ago, when fashionable people considered that to carry an umbrella was to say to the world at large, "I am in too great a hurry to shelter from a

passing shower, and too poor to call a cab if it comes on to rain."
Now, an umbrella is an indispensable adjunct of one's toilette, and I
am told that the *parapline* craze has reached such a height in Paris
today that the votaries of fashion would as soon think of appearing
in public without their hats as minus their umbrellas. When
photographed, they are taken in walking attire, so that this much-
prized article may be introduced. The gift of the season is an
umbrella, and happy is he or she who has an inspiration for the
handle. They are already shown with a tiny watch, a vinaigrette, or
a small looking-glass inserted in them.
QUIZ 2 *November 1883.*

*

A NEW BOOT

Bayne and Duckett, of this city, are now showing a boot which they
call the "Euknemida", and which is warranted absolutely
waterproof, without differing in appearance from the usual polished
and pointed-toed article.
QUIZ 8 *February 1884.*

*

A WALKING DRESS

This dress is of sage-green French face cloth: the bodice is made with
pleated bretelles, which are continued in ends, falling over the skirt
in front; the basque is very full and is pleated; long epaulettes fall
over the top of arm to form a sort of cape; ruffles of pleated black
lisse round the throat, finished in a waterfall in front. The hat is of
speckled green and biscuit straw, trimmed with damask roses,
foliage, and green silk.
EVENING TIMES *24 August 1896.*

*

AN EARLY CIGARETTE-LIGHTER

POCKET FIRE BOXES

An article of very great conveniency.

IT is so small as to be carried with ease in the waistcoat pocket;
in which besides the apartment for giving light, there is room for
a dozen small matches.

TO get light, nothing more is required than to take out the cork, and put in a brimstone-tipt match, which is instantly into flame.

TO labourers in the fields who like the luxury of a pipe; to centinels, to sailors on the watch; to solitary housekeepers, who may be out in an evening; to families in the summer, when fires are allowed to go out; in cases of sickness; to thousands in different situations; indeed to every person in some one situation or another, this cheap, easy, mode of producing fires, in every situation, may be a great conveniency.

Each box, price 2s 6d, will light a thousand matches. To be had, wholesale and retail of

J.A. TURNBULL,
Surgeon and Druggist,
No. 59, Trongate, Glasgow.

GLASGOW COURIER 8 May 1804.

———————— * ————————

BEN BARTON, JUN.,

Ladies and Gentlemen's Hair Cutter, Peruquier and Perfumer, Ornamental Hair Manufacturer in all its varied devices,

SHIP BANK BUILDINGS
No. 1, Foot of Glassford Street, Glasgow.

Respectfully acquaints the Nobility, Gentry, and Public, that he has opened the above Premises on a very superior style of elegance and convenience, solicits the honour of public attention to his peculiarly unique, and elegant mode of Cutting and arranging the Hair, on a principle embracing every recent improvement, brought up in the first circles of fashion. From the close, constant, and frequent correspondence he carries on with the first Houses in London and Paris, the public may depend on being supplied with the newest and genuine Perfumery, Brushes, Combs, Oils, Soaps, Ladies' and Gentlemen's Dressing Cases, &c., at all prices: Gloves, Stocks, Head Ornaments, Purses, and every thing in the Fancy Line, too numerous to add at present.

B. BARTON particularly recommends his inimitable HERBACIOUS WASH to Ladies and Gentlemen who visit the Watering Places, for immediately removing the injurious effects of the Salt-water; also, for eradicating the Scurf, Dust, &c. Sold in Bottles, 2s 6d; 3s 6d; 5s, and 10s.

Separate and elegant Apartments for Ladies and Gentlemen's Hair Cutting, and men of first rate ability kept for that purpose.

Orders left at 229, George Street, as usual, when immediate attention will be paid to them.

GLASGOW HERALD 4 June 1827.

———————— * ————————

AN EARLY WASHING MACHINE

SOON we will be able to do without servants altogether! A young housekeeper of my acquaintance has just been expatiating on the glories of a Morton's Patent Steam Washing Machine. According to her, you just put in the clothes, light the gas, turn the handle, and the clothes come out clean. Next to having clothes that never require washing, what can one want?

QUIZ 23 April 1886.

———————— * ————————

A NEW FUEL

HAVE you seen those new briquettes? They are blocks made of tar and coal dust, and they burn beautifully and make such a bright, clean fire. The fire must first be kindled in the ordinary way with sticks and coal, then the briquette is laid on, a backing of tripping put behind, with the result of a nice lasting fire. A briquette fire is especially suited to drawing-rooms, because of its lasting qualities and of the important fact that it doesn't make so much dust as a coal fire.

QUIZ 4 February 1887.

———————— * ————————

MATRIMONY

The hearts of the Glasgow population are turned wholly to matrimony. The steam-boats on the Clyde are unable to contain the marriage parties. In the village of Bridgeton upwards of 40 couples were united last week.

Plymouth Journal

GLASGOW HERALD 22 August 1828.

MATRIMONY

A MIDDLE-AGED GENTLEMAN worth Forty Thousand Pounds Sterling, possessing a Strong and Vigorous Constitution, together with a Mild Disposition, wishes to form a Matrimonial Alliance — Fortune no Object — Beauty Indispensable — Grace and Virtue must beam in every glance, and Love and Economy be manifested by every action.

Apply personally, at the ADELPHI THEATRE, on Tuesday Evening, Oct. 31. 1848.

GLASGOW HERALD 27 October 1848.

"A most attractive young thing."